WE COULD ALL BECOME
GENIUSES

SEEKING FUN IN
LEARNING AND THINKING

MITSUO OGATA

ISBN: 0991024001
ISBN: 9780991024001

Library of Congress Control Number: 2013922579
Duke Ogata
Barrington Hills, IL

The genius is an uncommon type of human being and the outward sign that he deserves the title is the scope of his imagination, matched by means adequate to its concrete and lasting expression.

—Jacques Barzun, *From Dawn to Decadence: 500 Years of Western Cultural Life, 1500 to the Present*

This book is dedicated to

the late Art and Maggie Smith of South Kent School,
whose dedication to education was truly inspiring and essential to
my growth,

and to

my late parents,
whose sacrifice to help me grow was too big to measure.

Contents

Foreword

This is a most unusual book, part autobiography and part educational thesis.

My family and I have known Mitsuo ("Mitz") Ogata since he came to live with us in late fall of 1967, his freshman year at Rensselaer Polytechnic Institute in Troy, New York. The story of Mitz's personal journey from Japan at the age of seventeen to an independent boarding school, South Kent School, in northwest Connecticut is gripping. It is a story of the great personal courage and boundless curiosity of a teenager alone in a strange country and culture and also a remarkable tale of how a sensitive student struggled with different styles of learning. Mitz is eager to explain how he learned in a new language and culture and to share his insights and experience with other people who take learning seriously and want to triumph over the constraints of mastering the challenges of thinking and learning. The reader is invited not only into his personal educational struggles but also into his needs for personal support and friendship. Mitz has no middle name, but if he had one, it might be Curiosity, writ large.

Members of the Dietel family hold bright memories of a young Japanese scholar helping to decorate Christmas cookies, a wild snowmobile chauffeur of small children over hill and dale, and a fiercely dedicated student who worked long hours not only to complete his undergraduate courses but also to learn German as he worked at perfecting his English! He was a big brother to our five children and a dependable child caretaker. His love of travel has taken him around the world, often on continent-hurdling jaunts that started with a "red-eye" on Thursday nights and landed him back at his New York office Monday morning ready for work. He was an uninhibited skier nicknamed "Duke," and he reveled in all the new and different experiences that life offered.

Mitz had to write this book, and the reader will soon find out why. He could not but share his educational venture, so sure is he that his experience could be helpful to others. His excitement over learning how to think, to analyze, to solve problems, to put himself in other students' shoes is palpable and endearing. Whether or not others can apply his insights remains to be seen, but there is no doubt that the story of his becoming an American will captivate readers everywhere.

William M. Dietel
Flint Hill, Virginia

Acknowledgments

Writing this book has been a great, fun experience because I was finally able to say what I had been meaning to say all these years! It's been a memorable experience as well, as I have felt endless enthusiasm from my family and friends in making this come to fruition. I single out my wife, Sue, and my dear friends Bill and Linda Dietel. Their love has been a source of life energy with hope and encouragement for my aspiration.

I would also like to honor Bill and Linda Dietel as my wonderful American parents. They took me as a live-in college student into their wonderful family when I was struggling with English. Until then I had been exposed to neither such a loving family nor an upper-class living style. As a result I was able to attend a historic and competitive American college and dedicate myself to study with discipline. I was naturally able to learn English of the highest quality, in particular phrases and idioms that tested my authenticity of knowledge with each of the family members. Over the years my social skill was nurtured through my experiences with their contacts, such as their friends, who were the top echelon of the business world, and their relatives, like the Van Voorhis family. A lot of what I write is a product of my life with them from 1967 to 1969 in Troy, New York, and the years leading up to today.

I say they are my American parents because they left me with such loving impressions, as only genuine parents would do. For example, one cool October morning in 1981 at 7:00 a.m., Linda and Bill surprised me by showing up among the witnesses at my swearing-in ceremony for US citizenship in the Manhattan Federal Courthouse. Writing this book is my humble way of thanking them for all the wonderful deeds and thoughts they provided me for nearly half a century.

I would also like to acknowledge the editing work of my great friend Tim Grant. Tim and I worked together in a consulting group within Trans World Airlines at 605 Third Avenue in New York City back in the late seventies. He was known as the "token WASP" because he was the only WASP in that group. Like a downsized United Nations, the rest of the group consisted of a bunch of foreigners and non-WASP employees. I opt to use the politically shaky term because his ability to elucidate any subject with enthusiasm was, and still is, both genuine and charismatically American. (I can still recall the time he explained the difference between *qualm* and *problem* with patience and clarity.) My wish is that, by rubbing off some of his quality, he helped make this book presentable at least. Without his help the exposition would probably have been a garbled piece in a second language!

In addition, I was extremely fortunate to receive valuable comments in the medical field from my nephew Dr. Jess Bouma, MD, who somehow managed to read my draft while working as a hospitalist in Tacoma and raising a picture-perfect family of three children with his wife, Rachael.

And finally, to my wife, who nearly lost the sense of her English after talking to me for all these years, I also wish to express my gratitude! Thanks to her patience and love, I have kept my sanity and energy to remain enthusiastic; she has kept the fire burning so I can continue my digging for knowledge, no matter how deep and how dark it appears.

It Is Fun to Think, Fun to Learn.
Really!

It Has Been a Long Journey

Like most people, I used to constantly struggle with learning and thinking. For example, I did not know how to think creatively and thoroughly during my early childhood. I did not know how to learn unfamiliar ideas effectively, let alone quickly. When I took my first IQ test, for example, it was totally unfamiliar to me; I knew I would not ace it instantly. Soon after my mother told me with dismay, "You are among the average kids." It was rather disheartening to be labeled like that because I knew I was better than that. Looking inward, I remember the feeling of accumulating frustration. I would blame myself; it was my fault. Sure it was, in a way, but I did not know how to do better. I kept reproaching myself: "How dumb can I be, not getting it, not seeing things other people can?"

But that was years ago. It has been a long journey, for I eventually "got it," starting with the discovery that the core issue was simply that I did not know how to think.

The "How-To"

What I discovered over the years is that it was mostly a matter of knowing the "how-to," to understand (I mean *really* understand) and how to think to understand. It was not so much the content as the approach to get it. I often wonder why it took such a long time to discover that.

For one thing, schools really did not teach me that because, justifiably and realistically, they could not afford to do anything other than the normal grind of teaching. Neither did my parents or friends because they weren't able to read my mind to see the roadblocks I had to struggle with.

But, like a chain effect, when I discovered the how-to of learning, I also saw that no one person was truly superior to others. If there was any distinction, it was that one how-to approach might be better than the other in quality, such as ease or speed. Eventually I became convinced that the few instances of results from an IQ test or an aptitude test could not justifiably be used to describe the whole potential of one person in comparison with another.

Once I became a believer in that idea, I felt less pressured and began to feel I was just as good as others. I was actually enjoying learning and thinking a great deal more. Sometimes the fun was hard to stop. On occasion, for example, I could not stop reading the *Encyclopaedia Britannica* because one topic led to another. There was no end to my curiosity. Before I knew it, the volumes of the *Encyclopaedia* were all around me, with pages open where I had left off! It was the beginning of my discoveries in the approaches of the "how-to." With the *Encyclopaedia*, for example, I discovered an approach to learning by way of asking curiosity-led questions.

Recalling My Discoveries

I said it was a long journey of struggle for me. Why was it such a struggle? To answer that question, I went back to the period of my transition in education, from the one I received in Japan (almost up to the secondary school level) to the one in the United States (the rest that followed). I say "transition" because I saw my education transform from one based mostly on rules and discipline to one in the United States that was based more on reason and volition. During the years that included the precise point of coming to the United States, I found some clues to help answer my question whenever I was able to learn with little struggle. Also, I could see various contrasts before and after the transition, which I found rather fascinating.

Why Talk about Them Now?

First, I knew that if I shared my lessons in a book, chances would be high that some readers could eventually avoid those struggles I went through. Not only that, but I feel very strongly that there should really be no reason to miss all that fun! As I explain below, the more enjoyable the learning became, the more benefits I got out of that learning.

The second reason is that I wanted to share my perspectives about learning and thinking. My perspectives are based on common sense, a curiosity-driven sense that I want to use what I have learned over the years. That emphasis has brought in such fields as neurology and psychology, with an aim for finding explanations for challenges of learning or thinking. It is not scientific by any means, but I feel I can contribute, however minutely, because of my exposure to various experiences and my decades-long attempt to seek more satisfactory explanations from a different angle. In lieu of the scientific rigor, I leveraged it with the "human rigor," a logical and comprehendible discourse. I have been on the science and technology side long enough to realize it is about time to introduce such a point of view to the perspectives.

The third and final reason is that I wanted to have fun contemplating future possibilities of my perspectives. I get excited just thinking about them because imagining the possibilities has no boundaries.

The Old with the New

Why do I feel enthusiastic about that—enough even to punish myself by writing about it? One big reason is that I see few champions rooting for the crucial cause—namely, that it is important to address the issue of basic skills of learning and thinking in daily life. More specifically, to most people, today's life appears to be overwhelmingly busy with things that do not emphasize the need for training in such skills. Furthermore, I see little emphasis of the need to improve one's personal character. Why is that relevant? The reason is that character, in my view, plays a key role in the activity of learning or thinking. Decades ago, while growing up in Japan, I watched the TV series *Father Knows Best*, dubbed in Japanese. Directly or indirectly, I learned how to learn or think in the American way (like how women were treated in families in the United States and how reasons were used in persuasive conversation). What I want to say combines these rather "old-fashioned" values with the new, with what I can gather from the latest in science and medicine regarding learning. To me, to think like that, or more accurately put, to *learn* to think like that, is really exciting. Naturally I am biased when it comes to drawing on old values: what I learned in my old country remains a big force!

Just for the Fun of "Digging for Gold"

This is a good time for me to mention the scope of this book. Clearly I am not qualified to make any scientific statements regarding the subjects of such rapidly advancing fields as neurology or medicine or psychology. What I say is for the purpose of raising the general awareness and curiosity of those who are struggling. My points are mostly the common-sense knowledge based on my experiences. I can rattle off some of them rather easily: our health is important for our neural activities, learning communication skill is part of learning thinking skill, and improving personal attitude can influence the ability to learn or think. All that sounds rather mundane, but whatever it is, I want to flag potential deposits of golden nuggets for learning and thinking.

Specifically the essence of our golden nuggets includes the following three actions: 1) realizing the importance of learning or discovering the how-to, 2) learning to self-generate that ability to learn or discover the how-to, and 3) extending that learning to further enhancement of the ability— not only to learning but also to thinking as well. The last action is challenging because it should be done with imagination and creativity. All this may sound rather theoretical but in reality it is not. In fact the reality readily provides the practical side of the point: the basic common-sense prerequisite for the digging effort is to maintain a sound body on a daily basis. With a sound body, it is not difficult to find the invaluable how-to because the key is to understand that the challenge boils down to practicing a routine:

1. Be alert to sense what is around you (*Observe*),
2. Be inquisitive to properly register perceptions (*Ask*),
3. Be honest to pursue your own purpose (*Confirm*),
4. Inspire and be imaginative in thinking (*Discover*), and
5. Learn to enhance each and all of these abilities (*Review*).

In the remainder of the book I will elaborate the above five points as a five-step approach. I would like to emphasize that the approach is not so much a collection of how-to steps as a set of inspiring *initiatives*.

Personally I have wanted to have a little fun, which is to think and learn while trying to communicate the ideas of this book. To me that is quite delightful because there is nothing more rewarding than genuine learning and thinking. Not surprisingly, I call that cerebral fun.

So here begins my discourse. I hope you enjoy the reading as much as I did the writing!

Seven Fun
Experiences of Learning

Described below are seven experiences during which I had fun learning. As you will see, they are not that unique, but I wanted to share with you some of the delight I experienced.

According to my *Merriam-Webster* dictionary, the origin of the word *learn* is *lira*. It means "to follow," probably as in following a person. The Japanese character (which is based on the Chinese character) is 学. The word is *manabu* and pronounced *ma·na·bu*. According to my Kodansha's Chinese character dictionary,[1] the character is based on a pictogram (a set of characters based on pictures) of an old man with his palms open to teach his know-how to his children.

---

1 Kaizuka Shigeki, Iwatomo Fujino, Shinobu Ono, Ed., *Kadokawa Kanwa Chujiten* (Tokyo, Japan: Kadokawa Publishing Company, 1963), 273.

From Obligatory to Enthusiastic

If my teacher or the old man is helpful, I should find it a breeze to learn. In reality, though, I know something gets in the way, and the effort becomes a struggle. Why? Yes, I may have little motivation or it takes too long. But even in the best of situations, it is often simply hard, not much fun. Why?

Some people seem to find it tremendously difficult to understand concepts in mathematics or science. Often, how to think is not clear, or is hindered by a mental block. With other things, there is no problem; deducing ideas logically is a cinch. In some cases, agony grows with the sense of obligation or duty, overwhelming any fun that accompanies the learning. Naturally the air of avoidance sets in, as it is painful. I have been there.

And I have come out of the misery, too. The lesson is that it certainly does not have to be that hard or painful. In fact, it can be easy and fun. Let me illustrate.

1. Physics in a Nonnative Tongue

My personal experiences discussed here involve schoolwork, like learning physics and English as my second language, and coming to the States in 1965 by myself at age seventeen. Yes, I was a minor and a minor could not have left Japan without an accompanying or sponsoring adult. But by some strange fate I slipped through the crack. Years later my father told me that he didn't realize there was such a condition on a minor, but none of the Ministry of Foreign Affairs officials reminded him about it.

In any event, let me start with a bit of background for a better orientation to where and how I began. I spent the first two years of my life in America at South Kent, a boarding school in Connecticut. To dampen their worries about my well-being, I wrote to my parents on average one letter every three days while thrusting myself into learning and studying. It was my way of staying in touch with them least expensively. International calls were forbiddingly expensive then, (in fact I had to wait four more years before I could talk with them.) All throughout I was dedicated and diligent, so as to continue receiving a scholarship. But I struggled most of the time. The first experience I describe here traces such general hardship during those years, both in living and in learning, shaping me to think often and think hard.

So let me back up even further—in 1962 my father was transferred to Tokyo, and my family moved to a suburb called Koganei. I was a ninth grader then, absorbing knowledge like a sponge. I often watched the state-run NHK (Japan Broadcasting Corporation) education channel on television, featuring an American classroom series on physics, dubbed in Japanese. The program featured real experiments using elastic springs and billiard balls. It was startling to see such demonstrations because my Japanese physics class had few real objects like them—we engaged in mostly theoretical discussions. Besides, the American narrator explained things in plain, conversational terms, which was nearly the opposite of my physics teacher, who spoke formally with a somewhat distant demeanor. The speed of the TV program was expectedly a bit too fast for me to fully understand, so I wished I could revisit it again for more complete learning someday. Little did I know that it would become a reality about a year later, when I began attending Kunitachi Senior High School.

The way the dream became a reality was that I discovered the school had a wonderful library; in particular, it had books written in English. It was really enjoyable to be able to handle and browse them. They were thick, full of pictures and graphs amid plenty of white space. The real shock came when I spotted the physics book, the one I remembered seeing on television. It really was the massive PSSC (Physical Science Study Committee) physics text.[2] As I skimmed through it, I was amazed how friendly the writing style was, with attractive photos, inviting graphs, and friendly tables throughout the book. What a contrast it was from the thin, terse, and stern Japanese counterpart, I thought.

I knew that the conventional writing style of Japanese texts was very academic because the students were expected to struggle in learning. The rationale was that providing intermediary explanations would be neither healthy nor necessary for real learning. The students were supposed to fill in the gaps on their own. It was as if the Japanese Ministry of Education had adapted the old Spartan philosophy of Euclid that there was no shortcut to learning (geometry). Or it was partly a carry-over from the westernization of the Meiji era, which took in the best knowledge of the advanced nations: the English political system, German science, Italian music, French cuisine, Dutch laws, etc. Specifically, the Gaussian quote "few but ripe" epitomized the rigorous academic style. So I spent a lot of time filling in the gaps with my own guesses (note "guesses," not really solid thinking). But I found such work to be taxing, without result, and, more to the point, no fun at all. It was annoying at times, too, as if the text were deriding me with that irritating phrase, "it is intuitively obvious that..."

When I realized how the PSSC text explained a concept with simplicity and fun, it was like a revelation. I felt as if it suddenly wiped

---

2 Physical Science Study Committee, *Physics* (Boston: Heath and Company, 1960).

out the sacred protocols of elite Japanese education aimed for high achievers. I began to wonder why I was forced to use the Japanese text, with its conformity to the social norm of formality and prestige. To be fair, there were plenty of fine Japanese books, of course, such as study aids, that took more popular and common colloquial paths. But why was I not allowed to choose a path of learning with fun and ease?

Soon after that library experience, I had one of those defining moments. I decided my goal was to pursue education in English someday. In particular, I was determined I was going to learn physics in English!

After a while I began to notice that *both* American and Japanese educational techniques actually had good qualities, specifically about learning physics. For one, the Japanese approach appeared to excel in teaching formulas and problem-solving instructions. When I followed the Japanese technique, I was better at homework tasks, with faster speed. They were mechanical, and I found the drill to be very useful. The American approach didn't really help me with such a *tactical* side of learning.

The American-style teaching approach for physics in English was great at explaining the why and how, which provided me with different explanations, viewpoints, perspectives, and steps to think more for myself. One characteristic was that it was always asking questions. Until I became aware of this learning approach based on questions, I did not value physics experiments because books were really the only media for learning. I was going head over heels trying to digest new words that were hard to understand. Within the world of Japanese books, there was little room for posing questions. Thought experiments and illustrations were usually not given in inquisitive styles. I felt I was not encouraged to question because

11

it was not a style of *elite* learning. The style was commanding and condescending or pedagogical. On the contrary, the PSSC text allocated many pages to explain concepts, like that of inertia, with questions, diagrams, and photos of experiments. Several pages later it led to one of the concepts Newton had come up with. I was excited because I felt I was tracing Newton's footsteps! On the contrary, my Japanese text explained the whole inertia topic in a few paragraphs, and Newton remained a distant godlike impression. To be sure, I was not blaming the Japanese approach; I just was not yet an elite enough student to appreciate it.

In any event, that was one thrilling and powerful revelation! It was not only simpler but also fun to learn in English because *the English language helped make it easier for me to think!* Of course, it was more than just the language, but to me the magic then was the English language. Later on I applied this in German (first from English, as I learned German in English, and later in Japanese as well). It worked well.

So here is what I found:

> *Try to look for different explanations, even in another language.*

2. Posing Questions Rather than Quoting Facts

Learning through questions was perhaps the greatest treasure I discovered in my learning, and realizing the value of questioning was the greatest awakening of my intellectual maturity. To many people that's an old story. However, part of the reason I discovered the importance of questioning so late has its root in the culture in which I was raised.

I grew up asking few questions in public because that was a sign of disobedience in Japanese culture. So I generally found it hard to ask questions, let alone good questions. Asking (and answering) questions publicly was often taken as a form of showing off, demonstrating a lack of modesty, and being almost uncivil, with an impolite demeanor. One consequence of such an education was partial ineffectiveness in learning. At least to those who are not familiar with the Japanese culture, I probably looked apathetic and indifferent.

Once in the United States, I had to break that mode, mold, and mind-set with conscious effort; otherwise I could not accomplish much. But that in itself was great learning—I had to learn how to go against the comfortable grain very quickly. My tactical solution was to prod myself to come up with questions in classrooms, meetings, and in public in general. That is, I *forced* myself to come up with questions. It was that basic, requiring special effort on my part, as I had a weak faculty in that area. Over time, of course, I did develop the skills, to a level judged normal by the US "standard."

Here is an example: In a computer simulation class I took years later, given by the late Professor Edward Ignall at Columbia's School of Engineering and Applied Science, I spent a lot of energy coming up with good questions and, surprisingly, not doing much else. In a way I wanted to experiment with learning almost solely by question, to see how helpful questions were to learning. Luckily, thanks to the professor's leadership, which encouraged questions, the classroom environment was conducive to that. As a result I recall I had so much *fun* learning the subject. My term paper had a lot of leading questions, whose answers filled the rest of the paper. Questions followed by answers, questions followed by answers...as if the discussion were carried out on autopilot.

Years before, when I was a student in Japan, that kind of learning method was nearly unthinkable, for the cultural fabric of "listen and follow the order" did not tolerate such a free and casual form of learning. Albert Einstein would most likely have made a ruckus and turned out to be a poor student in Japan, and he detested the regimented German teaching methods.[3] He might even have been regarded insane with his wild questions and pursuit of the greatest fantasy he could imagine, all driven by truth seeking and curiosity.

So first I had to convince myself that it was all right to ask questions. Second, I had to work on what kind of questions I should ask. Third, I had to develop phrasing skills of choosing the right words. Ed Ignall was always encouraging and patient. That was perhaps why I felt great in his class. The hardest part turned out to be learning how to pose a question in order to understand a concept. (Addressed by numerous educators, this certainly is by no means a unique idea.[4])

So here is what I learned:

> *Work on how to ask rather than how to answer. Converting a statement into a question often makes things easier to understand.*

3. A New Word of Another Language

It took a long time to realize that the words I chose and used in learning played a huge role in that learning. The following experience

---

3 Walter Isaacson, *Einstein: His Life and Universe* (New York: Simon and Schuster, 2007).
4 Walter Pauk, *How to Study in College* (Boston: Houghton Mifflin Company, 1993), 149.

was the beginning of such a realization. It began with an insightful suggestion I received from one of my teachers. When I did take up his suggestion and started using it, it really hit me as an awesome and handy learning technique. The insightful lesson was to get into the habit of looking up a new word in English both ways. What he meant was that when first learning an English word, I should look up the new translated word in the reverse direction as well to ensure the accuracy of my understanding. Let me elaborate with an example.

Suppose I want to understand a phrase, say, *a priori*. I look it up in an English-Japanese dictionary. Suppose I find its translation in Japanese. His point was I should then look up that translation in a Japanese-English dictionary to find an English word for it. In most cases I needed to go back and forth several times to ensure my understanding. The teacher's point was that the goal was not so much finding a translation as it was really learning the new word in its true meaning. Certainly the amount of work was greater, but the benefits were huge because it helped me remember the word easily. It opened my viewpoints widely by exposing me to the etymological origins. Sometimes I even ended up learning various facts in history, religion, and sociology.

For each word in a language, there is usually a corresponding word in another language, one for one—*hour, red, eat,* for instance. But there are also other words that do not so correspond. One word in one language can take several words in another language to define it because the word is unique to one language and not the other.

The Japanese word *wabi,* for example, has no simple counterpart in English. The closest simplified translation I have seen is "poverty."[5]

---

5 Garr Reynolds, *Presentation Zen* (Berkeley, CA: New Riders, 2008), 109.

The lack of a similar idea in English is due its association in Zen, which is not a Western idea. Another gap shows up in the conceptual framework of sentence formation; it is infrequent that the Japanese language uses an inanimate object explicitly as the subject of a sentence. The word *it*, used in "it is cold out here," disappears in Japanese because it is basically viewed as unnecessary.

Other examples include plurals and gender in English, such as *child/children* or *chairman/chairwoman*. Japanese has to explain them specifically as added descriptions, as there are no corresponding words for them. Moreover, certain English words are quite refined; for instance, *should* has about eleven different meanings in its definitions,[6] but there seems to be no direct equivalent of that word in Japanese as each meaning or concept of *should* is separately described by different words. Naturally I often wondered how it was possible for English-speaking folks to include so many different uses of one word.

In any case, with these thoughts I gradually began to realize that learning English words could be more challenging than met the eye because it involved understanding their intricate backgrounds. The origin or the lexicographical information, for example, was often extremely helpful, and I became convinced that I should read the origin for each new word I encountered. Sometimes it looked like the word itself was almost secondary in importance compared to how the word came to its existence and usage.

These experiences revealed a key to turning learning into a fun activity. They left a powerful impression, like a revelation. And I also got a surprise reward by expanding my views and comprehension;

---

6 *Webster's Ninth New Collegiate Dictionary* (Springfield, MA: Merriam-Webster Inc., 1983).

learning a second language helped me clarify ambiguity in my own native Japanese.

So here is my discovery:

A word is a concept more than a definition.

4. Pronouncing an English Word

This experience is naturally more relevant to those learning to *speak* English as a second language, especially Japanese students, but the concept, I believe, is of interest to everyone.

I began my English learning much the same way as most Japanese students—reciting sentences the same way my teacher said several times very routinely in a classroom. But it was dominated by learning grammar, the mechanical drudgery of formality and regularity. So if it weren't for my share of luck, I would never have known how to speak in English more authentically than most Japanese.

Here is what I mean. One day in 1964, when I was an eleventh grader at Kunitachi High School, my homeroom teacher, Mrs. Arata, asked for volunteers for an experimental English conversation course. With more volunteers than necessary, we ended up having a drawing for it. The luck I just mentioned was that I picked one of those winning tickets.

The English conversation course turned out to be a teaching experiment conducted by an African-American professor, Silas Mosley, of the International Christian University near Tokyo. It was called The Spoken English: A One-Year Program. His method was radically unique in that he believed he could best teach how to speak English by helping the student reproduce the native sounds of English. To determine the validity of his thesis, he devised a methodology that included use of a mirror and a tape recorder, along with a brief mimeograph copy of the anatomical diagrams of the mouth, tongue, and throat. As a volunteer I was to listen to the tape and study the diagrams by checking my own pronunciation in the mirror until I could reproduce the pieces of sound he recorded on the tape as closely as possible. Then when I was ready, I was supposed to record my portion on the tape and return it to him by mail. I was supposed to do it once a week. He did not really discuss much else, at least at the beginning, because he focused on teaching how to say those English vowels and consonants. Initially I was not at all impressed with his methodology. I kept feeling dumb and aimless because I had to repeat funny sounds over and over, looking at my facial movements in the mirror and taping my noise monotonously.

I got impatient. To check out what was going on, one day I decided to hand deliver my tape to his office in Mitaka under the pretense of tardiness. When I did meet him for the first time, I was shocked by his huge, obese physique (utterly the opposite image I had of someone with such a soft but deep voice) and the darkness of his skin (I had never met an African-American till then). But I was impressed by his knowledge and conviction about his idea. After that I realigned my thoughts to focus more on his basic thesis. As time went by, the degree of difficulty increased proportionately as he kept building teachable material upon previous lessons. I was eager and studied seriously. I could even begin to see the fruit of my work.

Today I am truly thankful that I did not give up or quit out of impatience or arrogance. In retrospect, the experimental course helped develop my automatic audio reflexes by coordinating body movements like the lips and tongue. In other words, pronouncing the words without being too conscious about it made it easier for me to learn how to say the words. I suppose that is what it means to say that a language is a native language. At any rate, thanks to Silas's teaching, I got a start further ahead than most Japanese students.

Now fast-forward about a year. I was a fifth form student (equivalent of eleventh grade) at South Kent School. South Kent, as I mentioned before, was a small (thirty-three in my class) Episcopal prep school in Connecticut. One evening as I stood in a bathroom of the New Wing dormitory washing my face, a classmate, Larry Newhall, came in to brush his teeth next to me. Hearing my pronunciation of the word *turn* sounding more like "tarn," Larry decided to help eliminate the annoying handicap. He persisted, and I stuck it out; we went back and forth several times, looking at each other and the mirror alternately. I eventually got it because I could see his pronounced facial, neck, and chin movements. Yes, it reminded me of Silas's facial expression lessons!

Fast-forward another two years, and I was a freshman at Rensselaer Polytechnic Institute in Troy, New York. I was supposed to be residing in the freshmen dorm, but I became convinced that I really wanted and needed to learn how to speak English well. So I looked for a family through Mrs. Evelyn Greene, who was a dedicated patron of the International Student Club associated with Rensselaer. I told her I was seeking a family that could put me up with free room and board in return for performing chores like cleaning and babysitting for the purpose of learning real English.

Enter the Dietels. Bill Dietel was the headmaster of Emma Willard School. Emma Willard, the oldest preparatory school for girls in the United States[7], looked like an impressive English castle spread

---

7 The school was founded by Emma Hart Willard in 1814 as Troy Female Seminary.

over a vast tract on a hilltop of Troy. He and his family lived in this huge (I used to get lost at the beginning) headmaster's house on campus; by more sheer luck here, Linda and Bill agreed to take me in. Tory, four years old, was the first of their children I met and was the youngest of five. The fate I could never guess then was that dear Tory would later instruct me with English pronunciation.

One night she was dead serious about correcting my bad pronunciation, particularly of the word *three*. She kept repeating the word, shaking her head in denial every time she heard my accent without the "th" sound.[8] She did not and could not tell me all that, of course, but she kept insisting I didn't say it right. Dejected, I remember getting really serious, looking right into her mouth and tongue, studying their movements carefully. Dragging a white bath towel around in the kitchen, looking more like a baby fairy, Tory just kept pushing adamantly. I kept trying, and when I managed to get it right finally, she beamed out a loud "Yeah!" with a huge smile! Yes, I did think of Silas again, thinking how fortunate I was to have had all those wonderful lessons with him.

So as far as pronunciation goes, I tend to hold the view that it is more a sound reproduction, like learning how to sing an Italian opera, than an academic subject. Stretching it further, that means if I were more musically talented (with an ability to read notes, for example), perhaps I might have acquired the pronunciation ability faster.

Why do I think "musical" to that extent? Here is why: Silas used another unconventional but brilliant method for teaching English.

---

8 In linguistics, the "th" sound is known as voiceless dental fricative. Among the more than 60 languages with over 10 million speakers, only English, Standard Arabic, Castilian Spanish, Burmese, and Greek have the voiceless dental fricative. [*Wikipedia* and *An Introduction to Descriptive Linguistics* (New York: H. A. Gleason, Holt, Rinehart and Winston, 1961)].

He employed singing in his lessons. I didn't know this then, but he was an accomplished blues singer (he was said to have later appeared on Japanese national TV and radio shows as a blues singer). Hence, he might have thought about singing as part of the method out of his love and knowledge of music. Indeed, he might have known much more than other teachers about the value of a musical approach. At any rate, in his weekly lessons he sometimes included his own singing, pieces such as "Motherless Child." His deep voice, singing it with the starting line, "Sometimes I feel like a motherless child," still echoes in my ears today. In those days I would, as instructed, simply repeat it and record my rendition. Listening to my work nearly made me regurgitate in disgust; without exception my part was completely awful. As I recall now, though, that singing process was amazingly effective in helping me attain the native sound. It was without pain! Trying to enunciate and exaggerate the articulation made me feel as if I were performing a slow Gilbert and Sullivan number in karaoke. So that's how I equate learning spoken English to practicing music.

To be more precise, though, it is not enough to have just a singing lesson to reproduce the proper sound. What it should incorporate, I believe, are greater facial movements, including the lips, the tongue, and the throat muscles at the same time. And all those sound generation activities, with movements, should be shown in their entirety, dynamically and graphically.[9] In part the fact that they are not that visible makes it difficult. I learned a lot when I studied those movements in synchronization with the sound, looking at my own face! The goal would be to do it till I could say it without conscious effort. As in Silas's method, then, there was value in the monotonous repetition—I was building natural reflexes. I only wish I had known how beneficial that learning technique was earlier.

---

9 See Appendix One for more on this idea.

Another benefit hard to realize till later was the ability I was developing to distinguish different pronunciations. I was slowly able to differentiate sounds that were highly sophisticated and developed, as in *turn* (whose sound does not exist in Japanese), or other guttural, short Anglo-Saxon sounds. (For more comparisons, see the list below.)

As far as learning the spoken part of English, Silas had the correct perspective; that is, I repeated and reproduced the sound exactly the way I heard it. It was not necessary to think deeply about it. Subsequently I learned to coordinate my sound reproduction elements, like the vocal cords, lips, and tongue, like a native speaker. It was easy to test the results—I just listened to how I sounded against the native voice. One sure way to improve was to keep practicing like musical notes, with interactive coordination of various muscles. Approached from such an angle, I felt confident that it would not be that difficult for me to learn to speak English like a native speaker. There was one catch, however—I had to keep up with my practice!

After a while I got in the habit of reproducing the English sound exactly the way I heard it without much thinking; I just did it, an audio mimic of the sound I heard. I concentrated on techniques to coordinate my "anatomy" both inside and out with audio resonance. The secret, then, was to deal with it from a sound reproduction framework.

So here is my discovery:

> *In learning spoken words, study the sound production "mechanism."*

5. Explaining Ideas in English

When I think about it, I see quite a few opposites in English and Japanese in several aspects, such as writing horizontally using letters rather than vertically using characters. Of course all that is well-known. But when I realize how opposite they can be, it is both funny and fascinating. For example, I have to position my subject and verb carefully in English, while I can get away with not doing it in Japanese. I need to pay attention to even a barely audible sound in English, but I can usually get by with a fraction of it as base syllables in Japanese.

I became fascinated by these two languages that are so far apart. So I went ahead and listed the differences. They are so large and yet not clearly known to the general audience. For that reason I want to explain the differences in some detail.

I would like to group them into three areas of difference: linguistic, conceptual, and cultural.

Linguistic

I have learned that English is guttural and "anatomical" while Japanese is phonetic, polysyllabic, and "inert." English dissects sound and enunciates it out loud, while Japanese nearly muffles its pronunciation. English has more than double the number of Japanese phonetic sounds, including the "th" sound and the ability to avoid lallation, the often joked about case of Japanese mixing up R and L.

Furthermore, the two have differing built-in rhythms, roughly speaking that of a waltz (tertiary, 1-2-3 1-2-3) in English versus one of a marching band (binary, 1-2 1-2) in Japanese. For the fun of it, here are some examples:

To get the English language's tertiary beat, try saying 2-7-2-7-6-4-1,[10] or "Get outta here." Or start rock 'n' rolling with those famous Bo Diddley beats, like "Hey, BO" (1996).[11] Now to get the Japanese language's binary notes, try a haiku. Read out loud the following oft-quoted piece about the old pond and the sound of a frog jumping into it:

> *Furu ikeya*
> *Kawazu tobikomu*
> *Mizuno oto.*

It should give you a feel for a binary, not tertiary, beat. The vowel-rich words almost force that no matter what. But if that does not convince you, try singing a folksy Japanese song like "Sukiyaki."

As a detour, here is my tip to those Japanese students learning English: sharpen audio skills. For example, try to pronounce the following five kinds of sound (linguistically referred to as *diphthongs*):

> *er* as in *ter*m
> *ur* as in *tur*n
> *or* as in *tor*n
> *ar* as in *tar*mac
> *ir* as in b*ir*d

If they all sound like *taa*, then there is some work to do with the hearing. If it is confusing, here is the how-to hint: differentiate the way each diphthong is pronounced. They are rather complex as each sound is created uniquely with intricate movements among

---

10 Linda Dietel used to cite this number over the phone very clearly, and the way she said it with such a rhythm is forever stuck in my mind.
11 "Bo Diddley," YouTube video, 3:23, andrewacton100, published on March 17, 2012, https:www.youtube.com/watch?v=zpvkq9n5604.

the sound-creating body elements. Thus, the key to real under-standing is to know how each vocal organ moves *dynamically* when pronounced. It helps to study their starting shapes, positions and the subsequent delicate movements of the tongue, the lips, the mouth, the jaw, and the throat!

Native speakers of English likewise will have a similar challenge when, for example, learning an Arabic language. The sounds involv-ing *kh* would be new to them, so they will need to acquire the ability to say them through practice, as with pronouncing even the more familiar rolled *r* in French or the German *u* with an umlaut (ü).

So the first contrasting point is the highly developed aural nature of English as opposed to the basic vowel-dominated Japanese lingua.

Conceptual

Now on to the second area. Conceptually, I note the English sen-tences are positional; by that I mean each word in English is placed in a specific "position" like the box of the subject, the box of the ob-ject, etc. Once a verb (a transitive verb to be exact, the verb needing an object) is chosen in a box, its object box is expected soon after it. In a way it is a mandatory pair. If I choose the word *remember*, the expectation is remember *what?* The word *what* is now in the object box. But the Japanese sentences are not restricted by such an expec-tation, i.e., not by position, meaning there is no box for it. Instead, a sentence needs a special flag called a "particle." A word with that particle affixed—always affixed at the end as suffix—becomes the object. If another word is mentioned sounding like the object, but it is without a particle, then the listener needs to wait for it to pair up the verb with its object. The object particle can appear late, even at the end of a long sentence. And I may change my mind by affixing a different particle to the word, making some other word the object. As long as I delay using such a particle, the listener cannot decipher what I'm trying to say. It can test your flexibility, patience, and even sanity!

For example, suppose I choose the following three words:

>*watashi* (I)
>*suki* (like)
>*hon* (book)

Also, I list two Japanese particles, *wa* and *o*:

>*wa* is a particle that indicates that the word to which *wa* is attached is the subject.

If I say *hon wa*, I'm indicating the book is the subject of my sentence;

>*o* indicates that the word to which *o* is attached is the object of a verb; if I say *hon o,* I'm indicating the book is my object of a verb.

So if I put

>hon + **wa** + watashi + **o** + suki,

or equivalently in English,

>book + **wa** + I + **o** + like, I am saying, *the book likes me.*

I can also say this by rearranging the position, like

>watashi + **o** + hon + **wa** + suki, (me the book likes)

In Japanese this is doable. That's what I meant by nonpositional. The key is that the particles stay with the same words as before.

Now if I change the above to the following:

hon + *o* + watashi + *wa* + suki, or

book + *o* + I + *wa* + like,

I'm saying "I like the book."

So the highlight here is the structural difference between the English communication concept and the Japanese counterpart.

Cultural

Thirdly, I note the *cultural* contrasts, a lot of which I'm sure are broadly known. English encourages exactitude and pronouncements such as in a debating posture. Japanese has nearly the opposite characteristics. Artistic vagueness and silence are treasured in Japanese; subtle statements are viewed as more intelligent, and harmonizing is preferred to differentiation and winning. Modesty is admired; flash is frowned upon. Loud sounds, especially those with exaggerated lip movements or tongue movements, are shunned by the reserved, especially older women. And swearing is mild in Japanese, especially in the sexual context.

So back to my point—being aware of those differences helped me learn English with a lot more fun than otherwise. I find that different communication methods or styles can largely be explained by these fundamental uniquenesses, even when the basic word for one concept is similar in both languages.

I used to feel a tendency to resort to images, that is to say, the eyes or video. Now in English I resort to the audio: I *listen* more carefully. So then I would imagine that English is better equipped or highly sensitive to unfolding and developing communication. Japanese does better in dealing with an instantaneous flash of images represented by characters. It means then that when spoken, sounds of English are highly developed in comparison and therefore need to be handled accordingly, in careful, sophisticated manners. Japanese, on the other hand, can probably contain a lot more visual sophistication than English. So I feel the Japanese communicate well visually while the English do better aurally. If I were to translate something from Japanese to English, I need to work on the diction and corresponding pronunciation very well. In reverse, from English to Japanese, I would probably be better off looking for a canvas and paintbrush.

So the cultural highlight here is the articulating nature of the communication style when expressed in English.[12]

The communication *methods* differ vastly as a result of these differences. In terms of trying to learn how to translate sentences, for instance, I used to go right to translating word for word. The better way is to think about how the sentences would be expressed in English more from the cultural and conceptual angles, especially the latter. The verbatim approach was usually harder and less accurate.

A good example is the English prepositions *on, in, at,* or *over.* The concept of *on* is attached to, not so much on top of. It took me some time to fully understand the concept, as there is no equivalent

---

12 This jibes with his statement, "Speech is a noninstinctive, acquired, 'cultural' function," in Jacques Barzun, *Simple and Direct* (New York: Harper Perennial, 2001), 142.

concept in Japanese. For instance, something can be *on* a wall as well as *on* a table, even though the wall is vertical; Japanese differentiates the vertical from the horizontal. Similarly, it took me some thinking to digest why "a program starts *in* January" rather than "starts *from* January." Why is a bump *in* the road rather than *on* the road? Where is the line drawn to determine if it is attached to and not inside the surface of the road?

As I recall, Silas Mosley did point out these conceptual definitions in a clear manner when he instructed us on the prepositional words; perhaps my maturity level was not ready to comprehend the concept clearly. But over time, through osmosis such thoughts led me to appreciate learning English from conceptual perspectives rather than from grammatical views. In other words, before I translate a sentence into English, I pause a moment to imagine how the native speakers of American English would explain it. So in translating a sentence, I seldom perform a word-for-word search mechanically.

One other tip: idioms, like *on purpose,* are great to learn because they give clues about how the concept is formed, as *attached to the purpose.*

So, finally, here is a summary of what I learned:

> *In learning my second language, I pay attention not so much to individual words as to how messages are communicated as a whole.*

This has become a rather long-winded discussion, but the contrasts are quite strong. I provide a comparison chart below for easier reference.

English vs. Japanese - Opposing Characteristics

	English	Japanese
Pronunciation	Guttural	Phonetic, polysyllabic
Rhythm	Tertiary	Binary
Sound	Highly developed and refined	Basic vowel dominated

	English	Japanese
Reading	Left to right, top to bottom (vertical focus)	Top to bottom, right to left (horizontal focus)
Visual	Alphabets, strings; appearance less of an issue	Characters, pictures; highly sophisticated, such as in calligraphy
	Strength: word recognition	Strength: pattern recognition

	English	Japanese
Messaging	Stresses precision	Integrates ambiguity
	Instantaneous messaging, as words unfold (direct, as in the Reverse Polish Notation: 2 Enter, 2, +: 4 shown)	Wait till end of the message to get it (natural order, as in standard notation: 2, +, 2, =: 4 shown)

Structure	Positional requirement (object position is expected after verb's)	Anywhere as long as affixed with appropriate particle
Subject	Almost always explicit	Often implicit
	Inanimate allowed	Inanimate usually not allowed

Mannerism	Tends to be loud	Tends to be quiet
	Pronounced, articulated movements	Discreet movements

6. Remembering Facts

Partly due to my experience with the Spartan-like, drill-oriented study method of Japanese learning, I was thrilled to entertain other methods that were often their rebellious opposites. If someone said, "go right," I would have gone left. Naturally it was a renegade joy, especially when I accomplished learning without such harsh drills.

One memorable experience involved memorizing formulas. I still remember how fantastic I felt when I realized I actually did not need to remember formulas because I could derive them from scratch. So I applied this principle to other "memorization" tasks. The key, as some people already know, is to understand and recall the concept in my own terms for easy access.

There are a lot of cases to illustrate. One is the conversion formula for Celsius and Fahrenheit scales (for those who know it, just bear with me). The concept is that the Celsius scale goes from water freezing at 0 degrees to boiling at 100, while on the Fahrenheit scale it freezes at 32 and boils at 212, an increase of 180 degrees. So the trick is to "associate" the two scales. For example, to convert from Fahrenheit to Celsius, first account for that difference of 32 by subtracting 32 from the Fahrenheit number. And now, to adjust the scaling difference between 180 and 100, use the factor 100/180. (To see it easily, just apply to 212. 212 minus 32 is 180. To equate 180 to 100, multiply 180 by 100/180.) That essentially is the formula. It is expressed as C = (F – 32) x 100 / 180.

Even with more complicated cases, like a formula involving compound interest, associating the principal amount, interest rate, and time period, etc., it's not difficult to come up with the known formulas as long as the concept is understood. What follows is mostly mechanical algebra. (See below for how Gauss saw the mechanical part.) Even if the mechanical part is lost, the recall is easy with the concept. And it's difficult to forget the concept once a full understanding takes place.

In physics, analogies are great tools for remembering details. For example, the size of an atom is hard to relate to something real.

> The atoms are 1 or 2 x 10^{-8} cm in radius. Now 10^{-8} cm is called an *angstrom* (just another term to simplify 10^{-8} cm as a unit), so we say there are 1 or 2 angstroms (A) in an atomic radius.

Try to remember this. Yes, it's rather dry. The definition may be lost in a few days. But now, read the following:

> If an apple is magnified to the size of the earth, then the atoms in the apple are approximately the size of the original apple.[13]

---

13 Timothy Ferris, Ed., *The World Treasury of Physics, Astronomy and Mathematics* (New York: Little Brown and Company, 1991), 5.

Now this is much easier to remember. In fact it will be hard to forget!

Another example from physics is a phenomenon known as the Coriolis effect. The concept, first discovered by A. Coriolis in the 1820s, notes the following phenomenon: suppose you and your friend are on a rotating platform, like the one commonly found in an amusement park. You are riding on one edge and your friend on the opposite edge of the platform. Now suppose he has a bowling ball and releases it to you on the platform. Even though he aimed directly at you, the ball actually curves and does not reach you. The strange fact is that if someone who is *not* on the rotating floor watches this ball movement, that person sees the ball not deflecting but *going straight*. As Coriolis was the first to observe that phenomenon, it is termed the Coriolis effect in his honor. A bit more succinctly put, if a person on a rotating platform releases an object to someone, the object moves *normally* (that is, without interference) to him or her, *provided* that the released motion is viewed by someone else who is not on the rotating platform. But to that person on the platform, it strangely appears deflected. So to comprehend the idea, suppose we have one platform, one object moving on it, and two people— one on the rotating platform, another on the still ground off the platform. The Coriolis effect has to do with how the object released from the platform is viewed by the two people. Each person sees it differently. Trying to remember how that can be explained is the challenge. Encountering a real experience definitely facilitates the effort. Here is what I went through:

> When I flew to Nairobi, Kenya, on vacation to visit my friends, Betsy Dietel and Michael Sands, one of the first things I did when I got to my hotel room was flush the toilet. Nairobi, al-beit barely, is in the southern hemisphere, so I wanted to see live proof of the Coriolis effect. As predicted, the water did not whirl counterclockwise, as distinctively in New York,

but was sucked in nearly straight down! But how does flushing it have anything to do with that?

Here the rotating platform was the earth, and the object released was the water flushed. Depending where the observer is on the platform, the object moves in a different direction. In the northern hemisphere, things that "fly away" northward from the equator were "deflected eastward" because of the earth's rotation, southward deflected westward. That deflection was what caused the draining ("flying away") toilet water to swirl counterclockwise. But since Nairobi was almost on the equator, the deflection would have been negligible. That I had to see with my own eyes, by flushing the toilet!

Here is an explanation of this deflection due to the Coriolis effect based on an article that appeared in Wikipedia:[14]

The Coriolis effect on earth is due to the fact that the earth rotates the fastest at the equator and does not rotate at the poles. A bird flying north away from the equator carries this faster motion with it (or, equivalently, the earth under the bird is rotating more slowly than it was), and the bird's flight curves eastward slightly (though its heading stays straight north). In general, objects moving away from the equator curve eastward; objects moving toward the equator curve westward. Moving away from the equator, the land underneath rotates more slowly, and vice-versa. An object gains (or loses) relative speed over ground as it moves away from (or toward) the equator.

---

14 *Wikipedia*, s.v. *"Coriolis Effect"*, last modified January 6, 2014 at 17:00, http://en.wikipedia.org/wiki/Coriolis_effect

In recalling this concept, I had fun because I did not have to depend on any memorization but on observations of physical phenomena. Using the same explanation, I could deduce why high pressures (air moving outward) in the northern hemisphere rotate clockwise (air flow is deflected westward), low pressure counterclockwise (deflected eastward), just by drawing arrows of air around them as movements. Resembling the case of the angstrom, the *concept* was etched in the brain.

Thus, I learned that concepts are easier to remember than formulas because of chained logic. The chains of events or notions raised my curiosity, often led by *why* and *how* inquisition. I found formulas and rote memorization not only hard to remember but of little fun, transforming them into mostly boring work or even causing me to drift away from thinking about the subject.

Incredibly, it took me some time to realize similar discoveries in each subject area, like "There are more effective ways of learning!" To some, again, that may be an old story. But to others, it will be refreshing or a lifesaver. Therefore, for the benefit of those who may need it, here are some more examples:

> **Math**: In math, especially in more abstract math, learning is mostly a logical building of assertions based on definitions. One approach I employ often is translating abstract concepts into something practical and concrete to "see," like diagrams. For example, consider the Boolean algebra. Like many people, when I first learned it, I had no idea how powerful the concept would be. How could such a "basic" idea be the foundation of the computer? So I tackled the concept from the computer's angle. I was impressed to realize there were three significant parts to this idea:

1. Boolean algebra: an algebra (which is a mathematical process of solving for unknowns using symbols in equation) that George Boole uniquely extended to a set of mathematical principles for logic (like syllogism) using algebraic operations (like "+," but with a different meaning, thus *Boolean* operations) on two (i.e., binary) elements.

    An example: suppose there are two sets of objects, A and B. If A is included in B (expressed as A < B), then everything that is in both A and B turns out to be the whole of A (expressed as AB = A).[15]

2. The concept of electronic computers: the digital electronic circuitry with on-or-off circuits. Their integrated circuitry was designed to control electric current to mimic the application of the Boolean operations on on-or-off electronic signals as binary operations on numbers expressed in binary expressions.[16]

3. The semi-conductors in the computer: the on-or-off (i.e., binary zero or one) information of both numbers and the Boolean operations could be stored in semi-conductors based on flow of electric currents through them.

---

15 E. T. Bell, *Men of Mathematics* (New York: Simon and Schuster, 1965), 433–447.

16 An Wang, *Lessons, an autobiography* (New York: Addison-Wesley, 1986), 40.

When I finally could understand how the Boolean algebra was applied to founding of the core concept of the electronic computer in its entirety, I felt ecstatic. It was impressive, clear, and fun.

History: I find learning history fun and fascinating when I try to understand the reasons why certain events took place. Linking the events' causality, like what led Japan to attack Pearl Harbor, readily opens up the window to the world scene several decades prior to the event. Details of various events, policies, names of dictators, and empires come pouring in with such explanations in the causality chain. Like the section on rote memorization I mentioned earlier, I found I could retain essential facts easily when I understood the concepts, or *why* certain historical events took place.

Chemistry: In an organic chemistry course I took during my freshman year at Rensselaer, I almost flunked a test or two. The terms were so foreign that I could not retain them in my head (*methyl, ethyl, propyl, butyl, pentyl,* and *hexyl,* for instance). It took me some time to see the pattern and system of how the terms were created. Most of them meant something. So when I understood the basic principle (like how many carbon and hydrogen atoms are in the above alkyl group example), things became rather easy. I was paying too much attention and energy to remembering the names for the sake of remembering, not necessarily for comprehending the concepts. Concepts in a way led to the naming conventions (for example, *butane* and *propene*: -an for carbon-carbon single bond, -en for carbon-carbon double bond)[17] .

---

17 *Understanding the Names of Organic Compounds* – Chemguide, by Jim Clark, last modified November 2012 www.chemguide.co.uk/basicorg/conventions/names.html.

English Composition: In English composition it was similar. I learned from several teachers and friends that the trick was to get in the habit of firming up what I wanted to say as if I were talking to the intended audience *before* attempting any writing. Given a period of time for the writing, I got into a routine of spending anywhere between 75 percent and 90 percent of the available time on the thinking part. For example, if I had the audience at the end of the phone line, how could I make it clear to them, simple to comprehend on their level, logically moving forward one step at a time, so that I could be sure they got my message? Once I had it organized in my mind, the rest flowed very smoothly, yes, with fun and ease.

Reading a Difficult Book: I used to avoid reading books that looked unfriendly and hard to understand (this book might be one of them!), until I discovered a technique. I still remember the oppressive feeling I had when I learned I had to read a thick book on Greek mythology. The technique was to check out the essence, like the author's summary or the table of contents or jacket cover talking about why I should read it, to get a gist of what the book was all about. It was like sizing up the whole task and getting mentally set to pace my energy on the whole. That made it a lot easier for me to digest the contents and to understand the intent and the organization. With that kind of forethought, I felt the book was now friendlier and appealing to me to read. When I got hung up on a word, phrase, or concept, I was seldom derailed because my interest was to pursue the main points of the book. Sometimes I even went hop-skipping the chapters or backward from the end of the book to grasp what the author intended to communicate. Getting the root theme of the book often needed this "helicopter ride" to see the lay of the land first. But once I took the control of it, rather than being controlled by it, reading the book turned out to be a fun adventure.

In summary, the trick is to focus on a full understanding of the fundamental side of the concept, and the formality, be it formulas or procedure, will transform to be your friend.

So here is what this learning experience taught me:

> *When trying to remembering facts, understand the concepts behind them. Focus on the idea instead of the facts. To recall facts, recall their ideas.*

7. Comprehending Complex Concepts

When I go back and forth between English and Japanese, I usually find English easier to use when analyzing things with deductive reasoning. I suppose that is due to conditioning, the fact that I came to the States relatively early in life. However, when put to review, some enlightening differences emerge with respect to the lingual and conceptual aspects of learning.

Here is an example: After I finished my undergraduate education at Rensselaer, I spent a year at Kyoto University as a research student. I wanted to compare myself with students in Japan in terms of academic level. When I went to South Kent, my knowledge in math was more or less two years ahead of the students there. When I began checking the academic level of Japanese university curricula six years later, the gap was not there any longer. It made me feel justified that I chose to study in the United States, so I was considering doing my graduate work in the States.

Toward the end of my time at Kyoto, I took an entrance examination to one of its graduate schools, the School of Applied Math and Physics. One question asked to describe the concept of the differential derivative. Without much hesitation, I decided to answer it in English because it was easier, more natural. What surprised me was that I actually *had fun answering it in English*. I felt as if I were presenting a paper to a bench of scholars, rendering my treatment of the subject step-by-step in a logical and flawless fashion.

English does have advantages of analytical aspects, in my opinion, for the following reason: its diction is refined through centuries of cross-cultural pollination. Look at the etymological components of any word. Chances are it has hundreds of years of mixing and streamlining through different cultures. But the crucial characteristic is its efficient sentence structure. The construction style is direct, logical, and consistent.

I learned to think in English partly because I found this characteristic very handy. Japanese certainly has the basic, fundamentally sound structure to enable analysis.[18] In general, however, when thinking in Japanese I found myself easily "distracted" due to its tolerant style and somewhat loose format, veering from a logical line of thought to a less logical train. For example, my thinking could go on without clear ending; I could reverse my statement dangerously and loosely anytime with a quick negation at the end. And, as I already mentioned, I could change a subject into an object with a flip of a particle.

Here is an example of a long-winded sentence. Even though it comes from a respected Japanese online newspaper, I have chosen to keep

---

18 Truthfully speaking, I must admit that when I do speak in Japanese for analytical discussion, I see that the sentences I speak actually do have English-like structure.

it anonymous in order to avoid getting distracted by the reputation of the newspaper. There are a lot of words between the subject and its verb (I underlined them for visual purposes). That tends to diminish the logical strength of the thought. It may be painful to see it in Japanese, but for those who can read Japanese, here it is:

焦点となっていた年金削減問題が、現役・ＯＢの同意による減額か基金解散で解決する見通しとなったことから、<u>政府は</u>、年金を強制的に減額できる特別立法を見送る方向で<u>調整に入る</u>。

A somewhat silly "verbatim" translation of the above is perhaps even more painful:

The focal point, the Pension reduction issue, seeing the current workers and the retirees having agreed to either reduction or fund closure, looking to be resolved, <u>the government</u>, aiming to forego a special legislative approach for forceful reduction, <u>enters into negotiation.</u>

In the above, the underlined words are the corresponding subject and its verb, as in the Japanese counterpart. Hard to believe, but when thinking in Japanese, my words used to line up in the above order.

A simpler way of saying the same paragraph in a professionally captioned headline (with a bit more info) by a respected American online feed is:

[The government] is considering an [optional] move to dissolve its pension fund for retirees if they choose to reject a 30 percent cut in payouts, according to a published report.

Now it is not hard to understand why I prefer English in explaining things. Thus, to me, English encourages and facilitates simpler and shorter sentences. How is that possible really? As we know, English has definite and indefinite articles, *a, an,* and *the.* The distinction between *man* and *the man* can be made in Japanese, but it requires different characters; the simplicity of the English concept is rather elegant and powerful. Singular and plural are distinguished; a native speaker of English can also differentiate whether a noun is countable or uncountable. The basic equivalent concept for the latter does not exist in Japanese. (Water, for example, is not countable in English; in Japanese, it predictably has no relevance.) Incidentally, why English requires adding an *s* to a verb in the third-person singular tense has been a mystery to me as to what led to it in the first place; but at least its time-tested rule is consistent, with few exceptions. I tend to feel these rules or characteristics seem to help make English sentences more *precise* than Japanese.

Another characteristic of English is the number of words, or shall I say, the apparent depth of its vocabulary. The diction, in the spirit of *The Elements of Style* by Strunk and White, or going all the way up to the level of Shakespeare, provides a high level of rhetorical sophistication. One measure of the depth might be the number of words that are classified in a thesaurus for a given word. For instance, if you look up *expedience,* the number of synonyms and related words appears to be higher than the Japanese counterpart. I would imagine we could run a statistical test to validate such a hypothesis, but the benefit lies in the multitude of synonyms with slightly different nuances. So once an exact word is chosen, it tends to be very precise. (A qualifier here might be that when it comes to social or cultural concepts of refinement such as those in a tea ceremony or hierarchical wording, the verdict may be on the side of Japanese.)

In addition, English can *logically* expand its vocabulary by combining the etymological elements of different origins. Consider the word *synapse*. It was an invention by Foster and Sherrington back in 1897, formed by putting *syn (together* in Greek) and *haptein (clasp,* also in Greek) together.[19] In Japanese, like German to an extent, a similar effort is made, but often it ends up creating a whole lot more complicated character set chained with other characters. Like the Roman numeral, it can get a bit bulky. An example of bulkiness is the following:

> One tree is *ki* or 木;
> Two trees is woods or *hayashi*, 林; and
> Three trees become a forest or *mori,* 森.

There certainly exists no single best medium, but in my view, the bulging growth in size and complexity is not really sustainable. Perhaps that may be why we adapted the Arabic numbers instead of the Roman numerals, that is, for convenience and utility.

Such a demand for precision and logic in English diction challenges us mentally, or to put it differently, English facilitates our thinking for coming up with specific expressions of questions. So in English I constantly feel a *pull* toward more precise, logical, and consistent thinking. The emphasis is directed toward articulation. Deviations from that can be an inability or weakness and often become unacceptable, at least in learning. Thus, thoughts in English become concise as they are driven toward clarity, logic, and precision. And that is one advantage or tool I deploy in asking questions when trying to understand a concept.

---

19 Arthur S. Bard and Mitchell G. Bard, *The Complete Idiot's Guide to Understanding the Brain* (Indianapolis, IN: Alpha Books, 2002), 80.

Another advantageous characteristic of English is the preference for simplicity. During my last two years at Rensselaer, I taught Japanese to a piano tuner in Albany, New York. Alden Crounse, a bachelor, found a great intellectual hobby in learning Japanese. Besides having a superb hearing ability, he was a stickler for details. He insisted on mapping English sentence structures to those of Japanese. He had a heck of a time handling exceptions to the Japanese grammatical rules. To him the Japanese rules appeared to be arbitrary at times, loose at best. Of course I could not explain why, often feeling helpless and frustrated. What was the thing that saved me from going insane?

It was the common call for directness through simple sentences.[20] Resorting to simplicity helped my thinking, especially in logical discourse. For example, as mentioned before, in Japanese, unlike in English, it is not common to use inanimate objects as subjects (or at least, it *was* not in my days! Today it appears that many foreign viewpoints are accepted and even considered somewhat fashionable to use inanimate objects as subjects.). As a result, the precise diction in English was compromised in translation due to the somewhat indirect use of an animate subject in Japanese. That often lost precision and efficiency. I had to use more words in Japanese than in English to explain a simple concept. It added more burdens orally, which was more evident in situations like a debate. The drive for simplicity, expressed in the shortest sentences possible, was a savior.

Again, the English language facilitates potent generation of logical thoughts by its simple, clear, and precise diction. That becomes a crucial key when posing a question. A useful tip I found is to ask

---

20 A simple sentence grammatically means a sentence with a subject and its predicate. An example of one predicate is a verb and its object.

in short and simple terms. Paraphrase it if necessary.[21] After all, Strunk and White said, *Vigorous writing is concise.*[22]

A similar interesting tip I learned is the telephone test I alluded to earlier. If the logic written on paper is not explainable to someone on the phone, it is too complicated,[23] so break it up!

Summarizing the somewhat long discussion, here is what I found from these experiences:

> *If I have a complex concept, I break it up into a series of simple sentences. That lightens the load on my thinking.*

Some say that's not news; Descartes wrote his treatise about that when he was sixteen! Yes, my discovery took a bit longer.

It is common to learn and then forget what we learned. In that respect, my hope is you had fun reading the preceding about learning.

Now I want to focus on having fun in *thinking!*

---

21 To paraphrase is to restate the thought of a selection more simply and clearly, to translate difficult, involved language into simple, easy language. [Reed Smith, William Paxton and Basil G. Meserve, *Learning to Write* (Boston: D.C. Heath and Company, 1963), 60.]

22 W. Strunk and E. B. White, *The Elements of Style* (New York: McMillan, 1979), xiv.

23 Brian W. Kernighan and P. J. Plauger, *The Elements of Programming Style* (New York: McMillan, 1998), 21.

Six Fun
Experiences of Thinking

Below are six thinking experiences I enjoyed. Before I talk about them, I would like, as in the previous section for learning, to touch briefly on the word "think."

Learning is work, and a similar thing can be said about thinking. An oft-quoted saying by Confucius is very apt: "Learning without thought is labor lost." [24] He did not say it, but thinking can be work as well. As with learning, most of us find thinking more work than pleasure. "Do I have to think about this *now?*" I can hear a friend of mine sighing. I will try to give him a pleasant ride now!

In Japanese the word for *think* is *kangaeru*, pronounced *kan·ga·e·ru*, and the corresponding character is 考. It originates in an ancient Chinese pictogram in the shape of an old man sitting with his head supported by his arm.[25] To me that is remarkable because the

24 John Bartlett, *Familiar Quotations* (Boston: Little, Brown & Company, 1968), 71.
25 Shigeki Kaizuka, et al, *Kadokawa Kanwa Chujiten*, 875.

character almost looks like the sculpture *The Thinker*, by Auguste Rodin. What Rodin said about *The Thinker* is strikingly descriptive of the behavior:

> "What makes my *Thinker* think is that he thinks not only with his brain, with his knitted brow, his distended nostrils and compressed lips, but with every muscle of his arms, back, and legs, with his clenched fist and gripping toes."[26]

I think it's amazing that the ancient Chinese pattern recognition and a French sculptor's idea centuries later converged into a similar pictorial representation!

When we look around, we see a lot of great learners and thinkers in history: Confucius and Euclid, Gauss, Einstein, etc. Evidently they all loved to learn and think. A stereotype of Einstein, for example, is that he loved to think so much that he cared little about how he looked to other people, wearing the same clothes all the time, often without socks, and not bothering to get his hair cut.[27] Bill Gates loved to think starting early in his life due apparently to curiosity and fun in pursuit of challenges for understanding.[28]

We can almost feel the strain on our brain when we try to think hard! By the same token, can we also feel the soothing comfort when we think about something we enjoy? What could cause the difference? How do those great thinkers really get to love to think all the time? Why do most of us feel we are not on the same page as

---

26 *Wikipedia*, s.v. "A. Rodin," last modified December 27, 2013, en.wikipedia.org/wiki/Auguste_Rodin.

27 Isaacson, *Einstein: His Life and Universe*, 427.

28 Janet Lowe, *Bill Gates Speaks* (New York: John Wiley and Sons, Inc., 1998), 4–5.

those great thinkers? Is there any significance to their success in life because they love to think?

The Quality of Thinking

Since most of us can and do think, in my mind what counts is the quality of our thinking, such as the depth, the extent, and the effectiveness. In the case of science, when I studied physics, the quality of my thinking was nowhere near Einstein's. Likewise, I can probably never emulate how Confucius thought in contemplating social survival skills and human wisdom.

So regarding quality, if I want to learn how to think like them, at least I can begin listing some key questions to pose, like the following:

> Effectiveness: Is my thinking adding any value to what I need or want?
> Purpose: Am I clear why I need to or want to think about a given subject?
> Approach: How am I going to think?
> Hurdles: Is anything interfering with my thinking?
> Physiology: Am I feeling well enough to think effectively?

I can strive to improve the quality of my thinking by working on these questions. But where or how will I get any *fun* doing such work?

To answer that, just as in my seven cases cited earlier in which I learned a lot of things with ease and pleasure, I can share my experiences. Here again I appeared to have fun thinking only after I discovered the point about "how." And like learning, once I learned the how, I had to wonder why it took so long to get it.

Here is an illustration supporting my point: Consider the Greek scholar Eratosthenes. According to another Greek scholar, Cleomedes, in his book *On the Circular Motions of the Celestial Bodies*, Eratosthenes is credited with having calculated the Earth's circumference around 240 BCE, using knowledge of the angle of elevation of the sun at noon on the summer solstice in Alexandria and on Elephantine Island near Syene (now Aswan, Egypt).[29]

The essential tools he used to measure the distance were:

- Camels to travel on

- Building structures like columns (called *Attic stadia*) to measure distances

- Water wells to determine the angle of an incoming sunbeam (here he evidently knew in 240 BCE that the earth was round from how the sun beamed into the wells![30])

---

29 *Wikipedia*, s.v. "Eratosthenes," last modified December 23, 2013, en.wikipedia. org/wiki/Eratosthenes. See also Randy Alfred, "June 19, 240 B.C.: The Earth Is Round, and It's This Big," Wired (www.wired.com), June 19, 2008, Retrieved 2013-06-22; and Isaac Moreno Gallo, "Roman Surveying," Nov. 3–6 , 2004, translated by Brian R. Bishop, http://www.trainanvs.net/pdfs/surveying.pdf.
30 Eratosthenes is said to have noted such varying angles of sun beams coming into water wells at different times of the year. With his knowledge of astronomy and trigonometry available at that time, it was perhaps natural for him to draw the shape of the earth as a circle. A good article to read is "How Did Eratosthenes Measure the Circumference of the Earth?" by Anthony Abreu. A translation from the original Spanish is available on the web under http://todaslascosasdeanthony.com/2012/07/03/eratosthenes-earth-circumference/, last modified by Anthony Abreu, July 3, 2012.

- Trigonometry to estimate the distance between Alexandria to Syene (he determined it to be about one-fiftieth of the earth's circumference)

It is hard to do this from scratch without any hints. In this example, even after we go through a basic understanding *with* hints, we still have to rehash and think! (I wonder if anyone is getting a headache.) But when someone does it and explains it to you, it is a case of, "Gee, of course; that makes sense! Why did I not think of that myself?"

It sure is nice to know the how-to. As in my previous examples of learning, I begin to wonder if discovering such information is the key to thinking as well. It seems that fun does come with it at least. As the examples below illustrate (Abreu 2012), discoverng the how-to facilitated my thinking by helping me set my mind for it. I hope you enjoy reading about them!

1. Dig Up Curiosity

While pursuing my doctorate degree in operations research at Columbia University in New York City, I roomed with a Korean fellow named Hyung. At the time there was one thing unique about him—he could not stop watching TV, even though he was in a vigorous and demanding PhD program in economics. Hyung, knowing he had to control his bad habit, tried a lot of both preventive and corrective measures. One was turning the tube so the screen would face the wall. It worked briefly, but eventually he went back to watching it. What did he watch? He watched mostly those soap operas in the early afternoon! At first I was surprised by his lack of willpower, as I was sure he needed it to reach that academic level.

Gradually, however, he watched less and less TV. Partly and presumably it was the academic pressure. Another factor might have been the conversations we had about some of the economic concepts and questions about them. We would talk about them, question some, and he would start explaining the concept, like the supply-demand curve, the utility concept, the human nature of greed, etc. He would write out differential equations and other mathematical expressions to explain them. I would ask him further, and he would get enthused about sharing certain beliefs he had with me. We always had great times talking about them. Often we could not stop! Our curiosity kept producing thought after thought. In my view, then, I felt his curiosity won him back his determination and zeal to pursue his academic work in economics.

So I learned a good technique to get me to start thinking about a hard subject:

> *If it is hard to think, I often take interest in the subject by digging up really curious things about it. Curiosity does require some jump-start, however, like what to be curious about.*

2. Judge with an Extremely Open Mind

Brought up in a tightly controlled culture, I was under pressure from an early age to mature in terms of how I was supposed to behave. "Don't say that to your teacher!" my mother would say. Or "Eat this!" she would command, pointing to a plain bowl of rice with awful tasting veggies and fish over it. Raised as the daughter of a Buddhist minister, my mother was the exact opposite of Julia Child. Folks from the congregation always did the cooking for her father and his family, leaving her with few opportunities to actually cook. She knew, though, through her college courses, which foods were good for me nutrition-wise, and basically she forced me to eat them, regardless of how good or bad they tasted. I naturally developed distaste for trying any of her cooked food and became a very picky eater.

But when I landed in the United States, all gates to a heaven of culinary tastes opened. It was like heaven because anything I was given tasted so incredibly delicious. Naturally I became adventurous; I wanted to taste other good food by trying anything that was presented to me. In the process I threw out all my past prejudices about whatever my mother was trying to cook. For example, I discovered the real taste of nicely roasted chicken for the first time in my life. I became determined to try anything people raved about, including some awful-looking dishes. To my surprise I was stunned by how great they all tasted, and I began to enjoy just about any food.

So I realized how important it was to think with openness, not openness forced upon me, but genuine openness from my own will. I realized that my past memories were hampering my trying new foods. That realization was important. My decision to discard the previous notions and open up to a fresh beginning was tremendously critical. It set a precedent of retrying anything I had had a bad experience with. Fresh thinking with an open mind almost always resulted in fresh learning. Yes, predictably, it was fun!

An extension of clearing out the old notions was to refute the mindset that cast those notions in such darkness. As a result I got into a habit of making a conscious effort to set aside the incumbent predisposition, at least for the moment. Then I made an effort to welcome fresh new impressions without any past prejudices. I began to introduce "reasonable doubts" to my own previous verdicts. I told myself I needed to seek the real truth.

How did that extend my thinking? It connected me with the renaissance mind of the West. It reminded me of the enlightenment of such scholars as Rene Descartes ("I doubt or think, therefore I am"[31]) and Nicolaus Copernicus (proponent of the heliocentric idea), who sought truth against the common norm of their day and the authority of the church. Oddly enough, for me, it took an adventure in eating in the new world to realize the value of such a thinking spirit!

> *If I find myself hesitating to try something because of past experiences, I make an effort to unlearn first to make room for fresh learning by clearing those past experiences. A breath of fresh learning is surprisingly pleasant.*

3. Search for Different Approaches to Learning

Earlier I mentioned my friend Larry at South Kent, who tried very hard to teach me how to say the word *turn* when my best effort produced "tarn." The reason it took me some time to catch on with the spoken sound was due partly to my education back in Japan. The culprit was how the Hepburn Romaji system was ingrained in my learning.

Romaji was a venerable invention by James Hepburn, circa 1887. He devised a systematic way to help express the Japanese sound in the Roman alphabet.[32] It became the standard, and all Japanese students learned it prior to learning English. One consequence was it impeded (at least for me) the learning of the English pronunciation. For example, the word *colonel* is "spelled out" in Romaji as *koroneru*

---

31 Rene Descartes, *Discourse on Method* (Indianapolis, IN: The Liberal Arts Press, Inc., 1976).

32 *Wikipedia*, s.v. "Romaji," last modified January 5, 2014, en.wikipedia.org/wiki/Romaji.

because that's how it would be pronounced based on the Romaji rule; a Japanese person would say it as *koroneru,* thinking that was how it would be pronounced in English. (Evidently Hepburn did not specify that his system was not intended for *English* words.) I never knew I was supposed to say *kernl* till years later. Despite these shortcomings, by the way, the Romaji system is still in use.

So one day I said to myself, "I need to abandon that Romaji method when trying to pronounce an English word. That awakening was the beginning of my rebellious act toward the old methodology. I felt good about that because I was now a level higher in my learning approach, in the sense of *how* to learn versus just learning—I was analyzing the *method* of learning, not the act of learning itself. I was able to see the learning as a *process*, the *how* to learn part, not the content of learning or what to learn.

Challenging the dogma of established teaching methods has produced tremendous results beyond my expectation. Yes, predictably once again, with a lot of fun and ease!

> *When I feel stuck, I remind myself I can always learn from a different angle or approach. To see if I am stuck or not, I ask myself if I am having fun. Seeking a better approach is exciting, and applying it to new learning is fun.*

4. Momentum of Contagious Excitement in Learning

First, a bit of history: I mentioned South Kent School earlier. My academic connection to that school began with Art Smith, who was a Japanophile. His love of Japan and her culture came from his father, who published the book *The Game of Go* around the turn of the twentieth century.[33] Inspired partly by his father's enthusiasm, Art made a memorable field trip to Japanese villages and countryside with his Yale roommate back in the thirties, when both were architecture students. He was completely awed and taken by the pristine, innocent, and refined culture of Japan—it might have been similar to how Frank Lloyd Wright was impressed by it, or even older than that, as in the case of how French painters were impressed by Japanese ukiyo-e wood prints. (One example of the innocence of the culture was the conviction of the samurai class that guns were weapons of a coward; they would not take up guns and stuck with swords![34]) But his career as a promising architect in New York City ended when his nerves were destroyed by malaria, which he contracted while serving as a major in the Pacific Theater in World War II. The end result was he decided to become a teacher at South Kent. Impressed by things Japanese, Art earnestly began introducing Japanese history and culture to the students of the Episcopal prep school as early as 1960 or so. Due largely to his interest in that cause, I was admitted to SKS for the school year beginning in the fall of 1965.

For me that admission was a rare and lucky prize—I was a minor attending a public school in Tokyo, and few Japanese students had opportunities for scholarship on the secondary school level in Japan, let alone the United States. Even fewer imagined going abroad for study. Furthermore, my scholarship amount was $2,150 annually for the full tuition and board, at a time when my father was earning

---

33 Arthur Rockwell Smith, *The Game of Go* (Rutland, VT: Charles E. Tuttle Company, 1908).
34 Noel Perrin, *Giving Up the Gun: Japan's Reversion to the Sword, 1543–1879* (Boston: David R. Godine, Publisher, Inc., 1979).

a pitiful $40 a month (at the exchange rate of 360 yen to the dollar). I became sort of an instant star at Kunitachi Senior High School.[35]

In any case, the first time I met Art was when he picked me up in his red VW Beetle in Stratford, Connecticut. He then drove us along the picturesque Housatonic River on Route 7 to South Kent. Along the way he used a word I did not know (I believe the word was *rural*). As soon as he saw the confusion in my eyes, he quickly pulled over. I was startled, with all my senses focused on his next move. I was even more startled when he quickly reached to the backseat and grabbed a large dictionary, a thick, beaten-up hardcover *Webster*. He looked up that word for me right then. With the engine idling, he took several minutes to explain the meaning and how to use it. I was grateful for his effort, although, alas, whatever he said never stayed with me for more than a fraction of a second. All I remember is that I was rather stunned by his direct action to take the time to teach me a mere word while driving somewhere along the scenic Litchfield County countryside. Later I understood his actions better because they were much in the spirit of the school motto (simplicity, self-reliance, and the directness of purpose).

Ever since, though, I made an effort to look up in a dictionary any new word I came across *right away* even though I was tempted to delay it till later. And I often wonder today if such a determined action plays a role in learning; because it maintains freshness, relative ease, motivation, and impressions, I definitely feel it is helpful. It's in the same category as reviewing what was taught in class

---

35 There was precedence several years earlier, involving a son of the Japanese royal family attending Kent School in Connecticut. His letters to his mother about his experiences there were subsequently published in a book. Some half a dozen students from private schools followed similar paths to prep schools in New England after that. Even so, few common folks had any idea about preparatory schools in the United States.

right after school. Leveraging the momentum of curiosity, fresh memory, and high interest does seem to make it so much easier to learn because it is so much easier to think.

> *If I had fun learning, then I try to use that excitement (enthusiasm) and momentum to go on thinking and learning some more.*

5. Thinking amid Distractions

When I was in graduate school at Columbia, I struggled with a lot of abstract concepts. The abstractions were sometimes so extreme that I couldn't "picture" any. I tried various methods. Some methods such as finding concrete analogies in the real world worked at times and provided helpful insight into the state of my foggy mind with a life-line sense of reality. The insight, as illustrated below, gave me a hint of how I could eventually sustain my thinking.

The beginning was rather discouraging. The abstract ideas tended to slip away into darkness as the chain of logical thoughts I built around them disappeared easily. Typically the first link in the chain was a series of unfamiliar definitions. Before I could fully digest them, they were already followed by a theory using those definitions. I had to deduce or prove the theory using what I was given, namely the concepts previously built that led to that point. But very little stuck. I was getting frustrated by not being able to proceed at a fast pace. Initially I thought it was because of the distracting conversation and noise around me, or the sirens of ambulances going by on Amsterdam Avenue. But that wasn't the case.

To supplement my living stipend, I worked part-time at night for a Japanese trading company called Toyo Menka on the seventy-fourth floor (I believe) of the World Trade Center I. I would take the IRT Number 1 subway train down toward the Battery around 11:00 p.m. from 116th Street. I got used to the screeching sound with gushing wind scented with oil, grease, and garbage that filled the subway tunnel. Homeless people and night laborers rode the train with me. I might call it a picture of the surreal underground of midnight Lower Manhattan.

As I had so much homework, I read my textbooks on the train. The amazing thing was that I was able to concentrate and understand the hard concepts I had had trouble understanding earlier! There was no real magic; I just had intense focus and determination. I asked myself a simple question each time I had to learn. My answer came quickly. I asked another, and the answer appeared quickly again. The chain of logic was strong and easy to extend.

That was what happened to me but I did not stop there to just acknowledge the possibility and to let it go as a one-time experience; my inquisitive mind now began to churn and search how exactly and possibly that could occur so that I could do it *again*!

During that time, I realized that the whole space of my mind was turning serene like a deep sea trench, just exploring and adventuring. The sound of the subway faded. I was amazed by how "silent" it got. Later I had two similar experiences like the subway ride. In both cases I found I could concentrate despite the noise. The first was in the middle of Grand Central Terminal bursting with commuters and people working there; the second was living in an apartment next to the Manhattan School of Music, whose students practiced their musical skills loud and free, including sopranos and trumpets, randomly from morning till night. Regardless of how insanely not conducive to study this was, I began to feel I could ignore the noise and achieve my goal.

In short, it was the act of intense thinking. Noise became music or even silence to my ears when I was thinking deeply. All the noise just vanished. With some practice, I was able to reach such a state of mind almost immediately, by will. How was that possible?

I trained myself to think about the concept I was trying to comprehend by building a logical chain. If I noticed a distraction, then I would acknowledge it, taking it as a phenomenon I could not control; I would put it in an imaginary garbage can with a lid on it. I would go back to the chain of thoughts, trace it, and maintain the path. I would ask a simple question to take a small step forward. When I got an answer, I added it to the chain. I continued by keeping a strong focus on my goal.

When I got annoyed by the lack of progress, I noticed that the real challenge was clearly identifying what was causing the annoyance. It turned out that usually the cause was my inability to fully think and comprehend. The noise was often just a scapegoat! Recognizing the state of my mind at that moment was the beginning. Afterward I was usually able to shut out most of the distractions around me.

Is this something that is difficult for someone to accomplish? Perhaps; perhaps not. In some sense it is a matter of practice. In a normal case, I believe anyone can choose what topic to think about, for example, thinking specifically about making some decision, say what is right versus what is wrong. If I can think about it either in a noisy room or a quiet room, then I should be able to extend that to thinking about more difficult concepts in a noisy room as well. I just need to intensify my energy to keep those concepts chained for easy access.

The reward I get from being able to take control and beat distractions is confidence—I can think about hard things despite distractions. That confidence grew in size as I began to feel "I can do just about anything."[36]

Thoughts that are chained in solid logic or memory can block out distractions to thinking. The chain helps me stay focused; I begin to notice I can really think.

6. Weighing Players' Strengths and Weaknesses in Team Sports

In 1973, after years of schooling and living in an urban environment, I decided to try living and working in the Midwest. The academic activities were replaced by immersion in the industrial factory floors of the Cummins Engine Company, filled with diesel engine oil and gas fumes. And the tall skyscrapers and complex subway tracks deep underground were replaced by a horizon of cornfields and the numbness of the vast farming land of the Midwest. Soon after the start of my job as a scientific analyst, my enthusiasm toward work life in Columbus, Indiana, eroded quickly. I began missing the adrenaline-pumping excitement of Manhattan living. One night I sat at a table in my apartment dumbfounded about the lack of it, feeling lost and depressed about what I would do for intellectual stimuli.

Luckily for me I found relief in athletic activities, softball and ice hockey in particular, organized by the employees. After participating as a member during the first year, I decided to seek a bit more challenge by volunteering to help the program with coaching and managing a team. I did that for softball and ice hockey. Did I ever enjoy working in such a capacity! The reward of having

36 Quote Mrs. Van Voorhis used to say to describe her confidence in me, "Mitz can do just about anything." See the section on motivation that follows.

responsibilities to get my team to win was beyond my expectation. Besides, the team included such executives as my boss and his boss. It was quite a shock to realize that I could treat them as my equal team players. My social life in the first year was 99.9 percent boredom; the second year, it was 100 percent excitement (though it felt more like 199.9 percent!) . Yes, not in Manhattan but in the Athens of the Prairie![37]

In both sports my coaching performance at the beginning was a disaster—loss after loss. I then realized I needed to think. The goal was to turn my winless team into a winning team. I knew it would be accomplished by neither loud cheering nor stern shouts or commands. The secret I discovered was asking the question of *how* to do it. Toward that end, I began studying each team member's strengths and weaknesses. After learning them I went through deep thinking about combination scenarios, like which member to put in what position in what order. The more I thought and prepared for such what-ifs, the better the results I saw, resulting in more wins. It was a search to maximize the chances of winning by placing players in the right sequence at each available point in time. That was the *how* I was looking for. Once I realized that, thinking to achieve a winning team roster and designing winning plays became so much fun. I was amazed by the power of such thinking.

This principle I learned regarding how to leverage the strengths of players, or how to think in that manner, has stuck with me ever since.

---

37 Columbus, Indiana is known as the Athens of the Prairie because it has a large number of buildings designed by famous architects, who were commissioned by a former chairman of Cummins, J. Irwin Miller, and paid through his foundation.

Winning in a team sport is a result of a well-thought-out strategy with players' strengths and weaknesses in mind.

So these are my experiences that helped me transform thinking from *no-fun thinking* to *lots-of-fun thinking*. It was truly fun to discover different ways of thinking.

But How and Why Does Learning Become Fun?

Learning or thinking is fun perhaps because of the sense of pleasure gained from accomplishing challenging tasks. For instance, once I mastered the concept of probability, I even looked forward to talking about it and its interesting revelations, such as the surprisingly high chance that two people in a group share the same birthday (in a group of twenty-three people, the probability that two of them share the same birthday is 51 percent!).

As for the deeper reason here for having fun, however, the significance is that I *discovered how* to do the things I was trying to do. That is certainly not surprising. If I know how to solve puzzles like a Rubik's cube, it is not painful to solve them. So if I am trying to learn or think, it should be likewise painless if I know how to go about it.

The hard truth, though, is that it is not always easy to discover how to do things. I suppose that is the reason for cookbooks and other how-to books. Conceiving an approach to a problem is very important and can take a great effort, especially when that problem is trying to improve your ability to learn and think. Normally I put little energy into that "conceiving an approach" part because I feel the pressure to do the primary part, that is, produce an answer or complete a task quickly. Is it possible to have an ideal mix of the two so I can eliminate the presumed pain that follows when I do not make an effort for both?

To that end I ponder the following questions about the how-to:

What was in the discovering of how to do things that made it fun? If having fun was significant in learning and thinking, why and how did it really become useful, for instance, to the day-to-day reality of living?

I pose these questions because I want to get to the deeper core of the conjecture that discovering such how-to knowledge is the key to learning or thinking.

In posing the questions, I first note it has the same manner of finding the how-to; I want to know how to find a technique to perform thorough learning and thinking. It is important to ponder that point because I see that it will eventually lead to seeking an answer to a more general question: how can I discover the how-to *on demand*, whenever I need it?

The Essence of the How-To

Discovering the how-to helped me because then I knew exactly how to proceed. Here is what I discovered with respect to specific actions to take for each of my experiences I described above:

Regarding my learning, the actions were to:

- Rephrase with my own words ("physics in a nonnative tongue")
- Query in a simple manner ("posing questions rather than quoting facts")
- Define my diction ("a new word of another language")
- Emulate sound reproduction mechanisms ("pronouncing an English word")
- Focus on ideas in communication ("explaining ideas in English")
- Remember ideas ("remembering facts")
- Simplify ideas ("comprehending complex concepts")

Similarly, regarding my thinking, I found the following actions:

- Let curiosity guide in uncovering interesting points ("digging up curiosity")
- Undo past judgments ("judge with an open mind")
- Discover learning ways ("search for different approaches to learning")
- Extend enthusiasm of learning ("momentum of contagious excitement in learning")
- Chain ideas for comprehension ("thinking amid distractions")
- Strategize for attaining real goals ("weighing players' strengths and weaknesses in team sports")

I see a crucial point here. It is a *shift in viewpoint.*

I say I acted to "consider the whole," not to comprehend the specific details involved. Considering the whole helped me shift my focus. That means my focus went from *viewing the details of a specific item* to *viewing the whole lay of the land.* In a way, I was no longer focusing on the details because the details were not quite important yet. The entire view was.

In other words, I was overviewing to grasp "what the unknown was all about" and not battling to analyze the specifics of the details. I was *discovering how* to shift my view of learning or thinking, from one of grinding work to that of a work *process*, in spite of the pressure to understand. It would be like taking time in trench warfare to see a chart of the enemy line when bullets were flying over my head and saying, "Shooting is important, but let me take a look at the whole situation" using a field marshal's eye instead of a foot soldier's eye. So the critical point was to *realize* that I needed to pause and look around, or shift my viewpoint. That was a key step in my learning how-tos because after that, I could apply the same type of effort to many other situations.

So what was in the discovering of how to do things that made it fun? It was the sense of accomplishment through freedom, clarity, and ease. I did it in my way freely and creatively driven by curiosity and desire to understand. I saw things from a higher ground, which gave me a sense of detachment or release from the pressure of finding an answer. From the higher level, I could see a path more clearly to the destination of the answer. And once the journey began on such a path, it carried me to the answer with relative ease. The experience was satisfying, and I felt more confident about my ability.

Then, learning or thinking is easy and fun *if* I know how to do it by raising the level of my viewing platform. Extending that point, I can even say that if I am not enjoying it or am having difficulties doing it, chances are that I am not really learning or thinking. If I find my approach to be unpleasant, then the approach is actually hampering my effort. Thus, it boils down to realizing I am not knowing an effective process or approach rather than I am not learning or thinking.

Of course, the reality is harder: it is not always easy to find the approach or the how-to knowledge because that in itself is learning or thinking! This leads to my next question.

How to Find Those How-Tos

In my early (say, preteen) years, I was mostly coaxed and indoctrinated into learning and thinking. I might call that a fortunate orientation into learning and thinking because I was lucky to have parents and mentors interested in education. Later on, it was more luck or circumstance—for example, I was given an ample opportunity to read books such as biographies of famous people and classic pieces like *Aesop's Fables* and *Grimms' Fairy Tales*. My recollection is that Japanese books were fun to read but, for the most part, less provoking to asking questions than the books of Western origin.

Then during my teen years, I gradually improved my learning and thinking because of my growing will fueled by my own choice of action: I was able to discover answers to my own questions, mostly on my own. I might call that a slow discovery of the method through my own chain of logic. Often I emulated others who looked successful in doing that. As expected, however, my efforts were usually restrained. They were limited by the permissible norm of the culture and society around me. If I had to make myself clear with my pronunciation, say, I had to tailor how I was going to do that to a frame of reference that the listeners (my peers and teachers) would approve of. At least that was how I felt. It was like trying to be a Roman when in Rome. I met their expectations and got an *A* for it. But I knew I was not able to do *true* learning and thinking freely to ideal perfection. As I grew older in my teen years, I seemed to have more and more internal scuffles with such surrounding constraints.

Naturally it took many years before I began turning my attention from working to satisfy general expectations of others to going beyond that to reach my own real goal. In doing so, I was putting more energy into tackling more general concepts of the *process*. In other words, I became aware that discovering learning or thinking processes was really critical. I realized that a process was a series of steps that led to the recognition of how to gain a desired result. For instance, when I was learning to write, Art Smith tutored me painstakingly several times a week before chapel. It did not dawn on me till years later that he was really teaching me the *process* of writing. (How I wish I could have gotten such a mind-set sooner! My only consolation is that he did see some fruit of his work eventually—I can never forget his happy smile at his retirement home in Truro, Massachusetts, when he saw some of my latest writings.)

Due to their valuable nature, I began accumulating the knowledge about those processes relating to how to do things. I did it mostly through applications of my own discoveries. Added knowledge went into my growing chest of life navigation tools. Gradually I became highly selective in their use. If it smelled like a potential trap of errors, I naturally sought other tools to avoid them. Consequently I improved on choosing criteria for how-tos. And, in time, I became a better predictor of the consequences of selecting a particular how-to.

For instance, it took some hard landings before I learned how not to take things personally. My old values tended to be too honorable for me to even think to blame other people or "systems" for any failures I was involved in. It dawned on me that the more viable how-to was not to jump to such a conclusion but to pause to think before making a judgment. The result was that such an approach for "not taking things personally" worked well, avoiding unnecessary stress and anxiety.

So then here is how I describe *my process* in general, under "normal" conditions; abnormal situations may include such cases as being ill or unable to think due to various disruptions.

1. **Preparing**: I get somewhat serious to undertake a task of learning or thinking. I might call that a "warm-up" of the state of my well-being.

    Suppose I take up the challenge to understand why hurricanes around the United States whirl counterclockwise, an example of the Coriolis effect.

2. **Observing**: I observe details around me.

    There is a low-pressure area sucking air in the Caribbean Sea. The interactive satellite image shows a whirl moving counterclockwise.

3. **Querying**: I start asking questions in a simple and brief manner so I can force out easy answers.

    The earth is rotating from west to east. I am observing the position from where I stand, in Illinois. If I threw a football toward the south and it kept moving for miles, would it show any curving movement? If so, how would I see it? Or, as low pressures suck in air, what happens if the football is moving northward?

4. **Assessing**: I then assess the answers in terms of their relevance to what I am trying to achieve.

> The football's motions can be captured in slow motion. Yes, if the football is in flight south, I "move" from west to east even though I keep standing in the same position, because the earth rotates. The football keeps going south, and I keep moving east because the earth keeps rotating: the football sees the earth continues to rotate eastward. So if I restart the slow motion viewed strictly from my position, the football appears to veer toward the west, getting farther and farther from me! Likewise, for the opposite motion from the south , for a football in flight north, the effect is opposite, eastward pull..

5. **Viewing**: Next I try to raise the level of my focus from the level of the specific details to the whole of zoomed-out view "above" them, intentionally not focusing on each object one at a time .

> I replace the southbound football with clouds and remind myself of the satellite (which is moving around the earth at the same speed, so I see it not moving from my view). I pause and shift my view from the details of hurricane winds to a simplified thought experiment—I imagine I am on the satellite viewing those winds from above. When I ask questions, I am able to consider the relative motion between the moving clouds on the

earth and me on the satellite. In particular, I recall the westward pull associated with southbound cloud.

6. **Searching**: I then seek paths of logic for the purpose of linking my questions and answers and trace how I discover the paths (assuming, of course, I find them).

>In that frame of mind, I seek explanations leading to my answer—"I now view the motion from the satellite..." For hurricanes in which air is sucked inward, the pull is a combination of westward and eastward pull. Eventually I discover the path, a logical link to explain the counterclockwise movement: *from the satellite* the overall counterclock whirling motion results. "Yes, that *is* how air circulates counter-clockwise!" Thus, the search is to look for such a logical path.

7. **Remembering**: Finally I try to remember what it takes so that I can use the knowledge in my next hunt for how-tos.

>Now I review how I discovered the how-to path. I realize that I changed my viewing position many times. I used all the observations. And I looked for logical links to connect them. I no longer deal with the specifics leading to the answer but with the process to get an answer. I will try this method in the future when I am faced with a similar challenge.

As I went through many of these experiences, I noticed that gradually I began aspiring for more and better how-to *knowledge*. The reward was addictive. At the same time, I also realized that the knowledge was slowly contributing to the building of my character, in particular my discipline. Take money, for example. It was my goal to earn as much as possible in a lot of cases, but gaining experience was my greater goal because with that, I felt I could always look for a job with more income. Such discipline in my character to aim first for gaining experience was a result of my improved learning skills. Some of my friends were in disbelief when I told them about my preference. Others might see it as a piece of wisdom. So, money or experience, which is more important? The point is that getting one or the other was not that important. Discovering how to think about such a question was more important.

Most of these are probably commonplace facts to many. Indeed, many already are probably aware that, in short, learning or thinking is to discover the how-to of doing it. It has just taken me a little while to be able to say that.

The challenge, however, is to discover the how-to on a consistent basis. So now I get somewhat greedier and want to extend my thoughts to the next level: how to discover how-tos for all occasions!

To answer that question, I believe it would be beneficial to look at other exemplary thinkers for any helpful hints.

How Did Great Learners and Thinkers Do It?

The question is simple: how did they do it? What defines successful learning or thinking? And what qualifies a person to be labeled a genius?

Consider Albert Einstein. He seemed to have benefited from his uncle, who kept encouraging young Einstein to become curious about anything and to question everything. At around age four, he was mesmerized by the needle of a compass his father gave him. By then his genius capacity was probably mushrooming rapidly in his brain.[38]

The great German mathematician Carl Friedrich Gauss was the son of a bricklayer father and an illiterate mother.[39] His uncle Friederich Benz, a weaver, was said to have contributed to Gauss's precocious development. Gauss had a photographic memory, but the rest of his genius, how he mastered mathematics so well and so fast, is mostly unknown.

The general opinion here is that events occurring in formative years could make a big difference in the formation of genius-type abilities. But there are many others, like Thomas Edison, known for having a "late" start. His well-known quote sums up his view of genius: "Genius is 1 percent inspiration and 99 percent perspiration." Perspiration aside, what helped him learn how to think?

The generally accepted view is that it is not really something one is born with but is developed over time—Rene Descartes asserted that it is more accidental than essential.[40] Perhaps it is the right mix of circumstantial chains of events that enabled the results and the subsequent adaptation to such events.

So then what do I mean by a genius? For this discussion, I define a "genius" to be a person with the ability to perform rare and creative thinking.

38 Isaacson, *Einstein*, 13.
39 E. T. Bell, *Men of Mathematics* (New York: Simon and Schuster, 1965), 218–269.
40 Descartes, *Discourse on Method*, 2.

Who decides it is rare or creative? The "audience" does. Gauss solved almost instantly at age ten a problem of summing one hundred numbers, each of which was increasing in a certain manner from its previous one. An example is the numbers from one to a hundred, or numbers in an arithmetic progression. He did it without any help from anyone, which was miraculously rare with any audience. The rarity turned up in his ability to derive a formula by himself.

The difference here is that I could not have known how to do that at age ten, while Gauss did. Somehow Gauss saw the pattern, discovered the principle, and created a formula to calculate the summation. That was his destiny. The rarity of Gauss is amazingly astonishing. My fate was to learn his discovery years later in a textbook. Now I know how he did it, and I could apply the same technique to similar things very quickly. I could emulate his feat, and if the audience was not familiar with it, I suppose I could dazzle my audience, too.

If I stretch that far, I can imagine that regardless of the audience, even I could still find new frontiers that are rare and original. In that sense, then, even I could be a genius. *Each of us* could become a genius, although obviously there are varying degrees of genius in learning or thinking. I see such variations in chess championship games and other academic competitions.

With such a thought in mind, I now want to look at some great learners and thinkers in some detail regarding how they did it. I have chosen four samples: my great uncle Manuel Inadomi; the Japanese statesman Yukichi Fukuzawa; two famous scientists — Albert Einstein and Marshall Nirenberg; and the ancient religious philosopher Gautama Buddha. I believe they were successful learners and thinkers. Some of them are well-known geniuses.

Manuel Kumanosuke Inadomi, the Entrepreneur

My first example shows how well my great uncle, Manuel K. Inadomi, could think. I came to realize his genius while playing a Japanese game with him. The first hint was that he was an extremely good shogi player.

I am not much of a shogi player (shogi is the Japanese equivalent of chess). But even with the little exposure I had back then, I could tell he was an exception. I hear a good player can foresee several steps ahead or is able to quickly react to unpredictable steps the opponent makes. When I played shogi with him, Manuel Inadomi impressed me with his superb ability. He was quick and merciless. He was like a master chess player. I could tell he thought very thoroughly even when he had such a short time for thinking.

What amazed me was that his thinking style extended to his grocery business as well. It was much the same, quick and thorough. I worked for him during the summer after my junior year at Rensselaer to earn money for the coming semester. Compared with some of the professors I had up to that point, I really thought he could think just as sharply and quickly as they did.

Manuel Inadomi came to the United States at age sixteen as a farm laborer—a lemon picker, to be exact, in Southern California during the 1920s. He followed his father and elder brother, John Kaichiro Inadomi. Despite their humble beginnings, both brothers became hugely successful, much like Horatio Alger. By age thirty or so, he (and his brother, *individually and separately*) owned several grocery stores, and by the time I first met him, his company had a chain of three large supermarkets. Somehow he thought I was a good candidate for one of his lieutenants, so he used to teach me the grocery business by explaining his thought process. He knew that such knowledge was a key requirement to be a future owner of his line of business.

Here are some of his specific points:

- Get your employees to do things you want by being clear about what you want from them.

- Do your work in business as if you owned the business.

- Whatever you do, be the best; be *number one.*

- Be alert and stay a step or two ahead of others by thinking far and beyond.

- If necessary, "I alone will fight ten thousand enemies." (This is a quote from the feudal Japan era, meaning, if I believed in myself, I would never yield even if the fight were against a majority.) [41]

Recalling his business style, I can remember some of the specifics of what he said, for example, about *making money.* He would say that just about anyone could make money by making one-time efforts. But it would be hard to make money consistently. Therefore, he emphasized that his aim would be of a long-term nature. That meant he needed to think not just about getting money one time, but also about building a business or an enterprise that could perform such money-making work and generate money continuously over a long haul. His focus was the sustained capacity of the profit generator, not the current output capacity or the output amount. He would say, "We need to think about

---

41 Personal correspondence with Manuel in Japanese, 1963 –1972.

what customers want, such as value. You cannot just copy competitors' practices. We need to think about what value we are to provide based on their demand."

So he would challenge me to think big, far, and deep. He wanted me to set the highest and greatest goal as an owner of the grocery business. The running of the business was not the main target of his thinking. He wanted to instill in me a fundamental gift of the entrepreneur's leadership ability: a habit of original thinking that places priority on strategic business actions and ideas. His favorite saying was that anyone could come up with ideas, only a few would act on the idea, and even fewer people would carry it to the end. He always held such a "far-and-wide" perspective, always with the highest goals in mind. Almost at any instant, I felt, he knew how to think correctly and thoroughly along those lines. Clearly his thoughts were all aimed like a beacon at his goals.

In particular he often expressed thoughts using the interrogative *why* in the form of questions, and others like *how*. It sounded quite direct and sharp, much like a samurai sword cutting through a shoji screen[42] to reveal unknowns behind. He had a knack for going to the core of issues efficiently.

The crucial question to me was, how did he learn to do that? How did he develop his ability to ask the right questions? How did he achieve such a quality of genius? He didn't have a formal education, but he was a very keen observer and listener. As far as I could tell, he was always asking questions, proper questions, internally and externally. It appeared he developed his thinking skill just by doing it every day, asking, in particular, the *why* questions constantly.

---

42 Shoji is a Japanese sliding door or room partition made of square wooden grid frame with white washi (Japanese paper) pasted over it.

It was as if he had practiced and mastered the skill so well that it became second nature to ask the right questions.

Will I be able to perform as well as Manuel? I doubt it because I lack the necessary drive and urgency. But in theory I imagine I could. At least I could practice it.

The next illustration expounds further on the value of goal-minded thinking. As with Manuel, goals guide the search for right paths of thoughts. But with Yukichi Fukuzawa, the goals were even further in that they involved the survival of a nation.

Yukichi Fukuzawa, the Statesman

Yukichi Fukuzawa was a nineteenth-century statesman during Japan's tumultuous era of transformation. In the face of the Western powers seeking trade and colonies, Japan went from the Shoguns' feudal society to a modern democratic society under a monarch in about fifteen years. (With a monarch, a queen, the United Kingdom, has a democratic form of government.) Why do I think he was of a genius quality? The reason was he was able to contribute uniquely to the good of a nation by encouraging each and every individual citizen to become *educated*.

When I was at Rensselaer, I happened to find some dusty and frag-ile old *Transit* copies, (Rensselaer's yearbook), piled under chem-istry lab tables. In them were photos of some Japanese students who were sent by the Meiji government during the 1870s or 1880s, trying to learn and catch up with the West as quickly as possible. Suddenly I realized I was studying at the same place almost a cen-tury later! It was such an adrenaline boost. I began taking interest in the history of pre-Meiji Japan with admiration and curiosity. One outstanding man I identified was Yukichi Fukuzawa, pronounced *You-kee-chi Foo-koo-zawa*.

What stands out here in Yukichi Fukuzawa's case is that he encouraged *learning* by the common folks so that they would become aware that they were just as good as anyone else. If they did not learn, he judged that they had themselves to blame for whatever consequences they had to face in life. And, if a nation were to flourish, he stressed, they needed to learn to educate themselves to become good, productive citizens.

Until the arrival of the European and the US delegates demanding to open the ports to them, the Shoguns ruled the country with their hierarchy of fiefdom. Japan was closed to other nations except for the tiny island of Dejima, which allowed the Dutch to conduct commerce with her on the island. At the time when Commodore Matthew Perry's black ships dropped their anchors at Yokosuka in Tokyo Bay in 1853, the country was like one from the Middle Ages.

Born into a low-class samurai family in 1835, Fukuzawa quickly matured as an enlightened leader for Japan. What guided him were his noble visions for the country to become modernized as a respected member of the world society. His exposure to the Dutch learning at the Ogata School and things of the West might have raised the level of his goals. At the least, he was awakened by the advanced nature of other nations. In the process he learned to think sharply, as can be seen in his autobiography. If not for his ability to think to achieve those higher goals, he could not have done what he did. Here again he was a quick and effective learner.[43]

---

43 For an interesting account of his life, see Appendix Two; a nice foreword given by Carmen Blacker in the *Autobiography of Yukichi Fukuzawa* captures

His high goal led him to encourage learning, specifically in science and the ideas of freedom, for every man and woman in Japan. Having lived in a hierarchical society, he saw that the common people had no idea about the significance of learning. If a man was born a farmer, he stayed a farmer for the rest of his life. But the whole nation was rapidly being exposed to foreign powers that were advanced and colonizing; he saw impending danger of innocent citizens becoming prey to them. With his renegade spirit of challenging the social norm, he began asking rebellious questions in search of truth and justice. Yes, he might have well been influenced by the enlightened thoughts of the West, such as the Declaration of Independence. And his refusal to blindly obey authority, in some sense, resembles that of Albert Einstein in his refusal to accept unproved assertions.

According to Fukuzawa, his ability to think was nurtured by his desire to learn, beginning at around age fourteen. By 1854, at age twenty-one, he sought to learn the Dutch (medical) studies in Nagasaki and the English language four years later in Tokyo. The schooling and subsequent trips to the United States and Europe led to his awareness about the vital need for the education of men. His pursuit of the noble goal conflicted, however, with the politics of Japan that aimed primarily at taking positions for material gain and power. So he remained on the sideline, and instead he devoted his energy to education. During the late nineteenth century, with his philosophy of pursuing real learning and thinking, his writing became a popular and influential force for the masses. Many believe his contribution was instrumental in bringing Japan from a

---

it well. With permission from the publisher, both the foreword and his essay, "Encouragement of Learning," are included in Appendix Two.

backward feudal nation to a modern civilized nation in a relatively short period of time.

Albert Einstein and Marshall Nirenberg, the Scientists

I now focus on two of the well-known geniuses in science.

In pursuit of truth, the thinking habit of scientists is analytical, using a clear-cut criterion of true or false. As I already noted, Einstein learned how to think early in his life. He began asking questions challenging authority. That was one of his methods of finding truth and formulating creative solutions. He attained his knowledge about how to search for paths of thoughts linking ideas and information, some of which included the following:

- Not to believe what he heard till he found his own confirmation

- To imagine freely without feeling hampered by existing conventions

- To lead his thinking by pursuing truths with curiosity (via his "thought experiments")

- To simplify thinking by analogy

An example of his enthusiastic and eager thinking style can be seen in his own recollection while struggling with the general concept of gravity. He was truly a master of creative thinking.

He hit upon the notion that there is no such thing as gravity, only free-fall. He heard his housepainter reporting he felt weightless when falling from his roof trying to paint. He was quoted as saying that was the happiest thought in his life.[44]

Among his many quotes, one epitomizes his philosophy regarding the essence of the act of thinking:

The essential in the being of a man of my type lies precisely in what he thinks and how he thinks, not what he does or suffers.[45]

It is significant to mull this over because that is what he believed about thinking. If it is this rare notion he came up with that sets him apart from the rest, I want to discover eventually how he built his capacity to think.

Another example of rare thinking can be seen in Marshall Nirenberg. He discovered that RNA was the carrier of DNA information. It was in the early days of DNA exploration when Drs. James Watson and Francis Crick discovered the now-famous helix structure of the DNA molecule. It is interesting to note *how* Marshall Nirenberg asked the questions and how he came up the with the right questions.[46] The excerpt is from *Scientific American.*

Consider the problem: the information inside a DNA molecule is encoded by the nucleotide bases adenine, thymine,

---

44 Isaacson, *Einstein*, 145.

45 Timothy Ferris, Ed., *The World Treasury of Physics, Astronomy and Mathematics* (New York: Little, Brown and Company, 1991) 589.

46 Ed Regis, "The Forgotten Code Cracker," *Scientific American*, Sunday, October 14, 2007. Reproduced with permission. Copyright © 2007 Scientific American, Inc. All rights reserved.

guanine and cytosine (A, T, G and C). The full sequence of those four nucleotides, which run in nearly endless combinations up and down the strands, constitutes a molecular message for building an organism. Each three-letter sequence of nucleotides (or codon) stands for a specific amino acid. GCA, for example, codes for alanine, one of the twenty different amino acids found in animal organisms. Cellular machinery strings together the amino acids to form the proteins that make up a living being. The task of deciphering the genetic code, then, was reduced to the problem of finding out which exact three-letter sequences stood for which precise amino acid.

In 1955 Crick himself tried to solve the problem, not by experimenting but essentially by thinking, just as a cryptanalyst might try to crack a coded message. He got nowhere and abandoned the attempt. (People today may attribute the discovery of the code to Crick because of his theoretical efforts and because in 1966, based on the experiments of others, he drew up one of the first charts of the complete code.)

Nirenberg started work on the code around 1960, but he had to confront a preliminary problem first. "My question was, is DNA read directly to protein?" DNA, he knew, resided in the cell nucleus, whereas protein synthesis took place in the cytoplasm [outside the nucleus.] Therefore, either DNA itself exited the nucleus, or some intermediate molecule did—what we now know as messenger RNA. "So the question I was asking was, Does messenger RNA exist? And I thought if I made a cell-free protein-synthesizing system from E. coli and added DNA to it, or RNA, then I would see if they stimulated protein synthesis."

The so-called cell-free system is one of the stranger tools of experimental biology. Also known as cell sap, it is a mass of cells denuded of their membranes, the result being a quantity of free cytoplasm in which the original cellular organelles and other structures remain largely intact and functional. In late 1960 Nirenberg and Heinrich Matthaei, who had joined Nirenberg's lab, found that putting RNA into the cell-free system caused it to synthesize proteins but that adding DNA did not.

RNA, then, was the molecule that directed protein production. At some point Nirenberg hypothesized that if he could introduce a specific, known RNA triplet into a cell-free system, and if the system responded by synthesizing a distinct amino acid, then he would have a key to unlocking the genetic code. Others at the NIH [National Institute of Health] were making strings of synthetic nucleotides, long-chain molecules that repeated the same base: AAAAA...(also known as poly-A); TTTTT...(poly-T); and so on.

Nirenberg got hold of a quantity of poly-U (in RNA, uracil replaces DNA's thymine), and he wrote up an experimental protocol for Matthaei to carry out. And so it happened that late one night in May 1961, Matthaei added a quantity of poly-U into a cell-free system.

It was a historic moment: the cell sap reacted by churning out the amino acid phenylalanine. One codon had been deciphered, and the triplet UUU became the first word in the chemical dictionary of life.

"That was really staggering," Nirenberg recalls today.

BUT HOW AND WHY DOES LEARNING BECOME FUN?

Had I been in Nirenberg's shoes, would I have been on that path of asking the right question? Most likely not, since so many renowned scientists were tackling the problem at that time. The majority's approach was to identify which code corresponded to the production of which substance. The problem was that the number of possible combinations was astronomical.

Nirenberg's approach was the following:

1. He knew that with RNA the cell sap enabled synthesizing of proteins.
2. He asked, if the RNA sequences carried the "instructions," then would putting an RNA sequence in a cell sap trigger a decoding or translation of the instructions to produce proteins?
3. So he put a poly-uracil RNA sequence in a cell sap to see which protein it would synthesize, just once. He did not have to try, like other scientists, to check each result of billions of combinations methodically one at a time.

The result was that it synthesized only the amino acid phenylalanine. Hence, he found the first genetic correspondence: RNA's sequence code, UUU, carried instructions to produce phenylalanine. *UUU* was the *genetic code* to trigger the production of phenylalanine.

The next example is another one of genius quality, I believe, because of the quality of the hard (philosophical) questions he posed and his ability to think uniquely on his own so far out of the ordinary.

Gautama Buddha, the Philosopher

Without anyone openly guiding him, Gautama Buddha was able to come up with some of the most fundamental notions about human life.

Buddha exchanged his kingdom for answers. Born an Indian king around the sixth century BCE, he abdicated his throne and left home for a journey to seek the truth and to answer his questions. One key question was why there was so much suffering in life. He pondered such questions by meditating all day and all night, supposedly in a yoga-like posture. (Can you imagine how painful that might have been?) When he found his answers, he allegedly became "enlightened"; that is, he could see things clearly and had answers to all sorts of questions. Eventually his thoughts formed a basis for the philosophical and religious discipline called Buddhism. Here is an example of his answers:

- No one saves us but ourselves. No one can and no one may. We ourselves must walk the path.[47]

I wanted to select this genius from a nonscientific field to see how his rare thinking and learning ability might be viewed in comparison with other geniuses in science. His thinking did not use a scientific analysis but a logical deduction. Can anyone today, I wonder, match his thinking performance? Perhaps not. Not in the sense of inability but in the sense of nonnecessity—because today much of what people do is so specialized and convenient, few would even attempt it. Chances are I would go to someone who would do the thinking for me or do a search on the Internet and use available information. I would not think of starting from scratch or reinventing the wheel.

---

47 David Rubel, ed., *The Bedside Baccalaureate* (New York: Agincourt Press Book, 2008), 112.

Another point is he was not from the West. I would love to trace how he came up with those questions and how he was able to find their answers in his antiquated day, without the help of science and technology, without a push by the friend or foe of modern capitalism. Perhaps he was influenced at the time by the older philosophy and religion, Jainism, which goes back to the ninth century BCE. Thus, Gautama Buddha represents a great learner and thinker of those schools of ancient philosophy, much like Socrates and Plato of the ancient Greeks. His dedication and determination to seek truth was so extremely rare, genuine, and strong that he willingly sacrificed everything he owned, including his own kingdom, in order to find it.

Back to the Steps for Finding How-Tos

So that is a quick sampling of a few of the great learners and thinkers. The natural question now is, "What is my assessment of all the things I talked about?" The original question was, "How did their learning become fun?" Or, how did they do it to make it fun?

First, here are some findings:

- Knowing a how-to makes things easy like following a cookbook.
- Results of applying a how-to are usually a success, making it fun.
- Finding your own how-tos becomes fun, like a treasure hunt.
- Coming up with good questions is a creative and fun process.
- Finding specific answers is usually not the real solution; finding how-tos is.

- Applying a how-to relieves the pressure of finding answers.
- The how-tos applied reflect the scope of the goal or the purpose.

These then lead to the next questions: How can I actually find how-tos when I need them? How did the greats above accomplish that?

It appears that the seven steps I outlined earlier for discovering the how-to can also explain how those greats were able to deliver their unique performances. To fully answer the questions above, I would like to go further with those steps. It is critical to fully understand that this is an approach; it is like an engine that can produce, not a set of specific answers to a given question, but the how-tos that will enable thinking and learning for the answers.

The Meaning of "Discovering How to Do It"

I stated that discovering a how-to is the key to successful learning and thinking because the discovery makes learning and thinking easy and fun. When I find it easy and fun, I know I am learning and thinking well. When that happens, I know how to capture the steps for placing the *new* (unknowns) among the *old* (knowns); that is, I have a process of relating the new to the old. The new is what I want to learn or think about. The old is what I already know in my memory.

A good example is learning to be a writer, as mentioned before. Specific words are the details. The work of outlining the ideas and organizing them for the desired audience is the *process*. Once I learn the process, it becomes easy and fun. Thinking is like writing in that respect. The secret is learning *how* the outlining process builds the writing.

Another good example is learning how to think. Consider my Uncle Manuel, who learned quickly; it was not so much the details of making money that mattered as *processing* or strategic handling of steps to relate the *new* (how to survive and succeed as "number one" in the United States) to the *old* (aiming for the highest goal, sharpening eyes, predicting consequences ahead, and getting people to perform their jobs, as he did in his old country—he was a self-described leader of a local gang, implying not the violent nature but the skillful nature that he used to mobilize manpower to his gain).

The trick, again, is to focus on the *process of handling* the new unknowns (what I want to learn or think), not on the *specific comprehension* of the details (of what they are). The knowledge about the process is applicable to other situations, but the knowledge about comprehending specifics is usually not.

Those examples of the great ones above seem to endorse such an assertion. Their thinking level is "higher" in that they are not focused so much on the details as on the process. Manuel was serious about making money, but he was focused on the process of *continuously* generating money, not on a one-time incident of receiving money. Because the process is applicable to other challenging situations of learning and thinking, *focusing on such a process* facilitates success. The level of consistency that those greats always deliver is part of what sets them apart—they can focus repeatedly on a process anytime, anywhere.

In short, then, the meaning of discovering "how to do it" is enabling an understanding of what sequential steps it takes to do it and what purpose each step is supposed to lead to in order to achieve desired results. With that enabled realization, the "fun" part begins because such a set of sequential steps, or a process, will lead to a lessening of the pressure of obtaining immediate answers or the usual pain that accompanies learning and thinking. The benefit of focusing on the process is to shift the attention from trying to find an answer (the "what" part) under pressure to trying to first understand the bigger picture of the process (the "how" part) with desire. That desire is the key factor for triggering the sense of pleasure.

The Ingredients Essential to the Process

But now, exactly what do I need to have to enable such a process to facilitate smooth learning or thinking? What are its ingredients? And what does it take to install in me the knowledge of the process? More hard work?

First, to tackle these questions, I note the following three items are the pillars that support the process. Not surprisingly they are rather ordinary items with little mystery about them. They are:

- **Wellness** of the body: I need my *health* to enable the activities of discovering the "how-to" of learning or thinking.

- **Exploring** in freedom: I need a good *environment* devoid of inhibiting constraints to execute the search for ideas.

- **Desire** to grow: I need my *drive* to provide energy to identify my purposes and dreams so that I can aspire to gain greater rewards.

Here are some additional explanations to elaborate on the above:

By **health**, I mean the infrastructure of the body and mind. Am I capable of learning or thinking like a healthy person? Can I access my words and ideas without mental or physical handicaps? Clearly I need, among other things, good health or wellness to be enthusiastic about taking on the task. That means I have both my mental and physical conditions in ready shape for learning or thinking.

By **environment**, I mean the orientation that is conducive to learning or thinking. It may include any mentors who champion me to learn or think well. It is an environment where I can access my words and ideas easily to help form my questions and recruit my imagination. I can pay attention to what surrounds me without restrictions. I can be curious about how things work with little constraint. I can express myself without fear of backlash.

By **drive**, I mean the dynamo that is needed to support my genuine wish to do better. I apply the words and ideas that I learned to culture my thoughts. I search and connect words and ideas so that I can understand them in my own way, according to my own will. I want to drive myself to select the best connecting paths guided by the criteria of my choice. I am eager to seek paths in line with my purpose. Specifically, I want to look for those "how-to paths" that will lead me to my goal. I want to choose those paths that agree with my desire to improve and contribute to my overall benefit. I want to improve myself and my character so that I can reap more rewards. For all that, I need a strong drive to be genuine about why I want to do it.

Let me illustrate:

When I begin a task, mental or physical, I often conduct a quick test regarding my physical coordination. The test could be as simple as tossing a piece of used tissue into a wastebasket. If I pass the test by throwing it into the basket, I know I have a good overall starting basis. An example is the pronouncing of words. My lips have to move. My mind has to be alert to orchestrate all of what I learned. It is a culmination of the physical motion of lips to produce the right vowels and consonants with good mental coordination.

I was able to make use of this testing idea when I was working on my doctoral thesis. Some nights new points of view would come up when I felt loose in the ability to shift perspectives or paradigms, as if I were making a move to throw a basketball into the hoop. The flexible or creative move was a close parallel to the creative action to view ideas differently to come up with various theorems. When I got stuck with no further ideas, I reminded myself to be loose and creative; to my surprise, it worked quite often. Furthermore, the feeling of confidence sent signals to the neural network, echoing what Mrs. Van Voorhis used to say to introduce me to her acquaintances: "Mitz can do just about anything!" I certainly felt I had my environment and drive under my own control!

The corollary I use even today is that if I am not feeling like I could do just about anything, I take it as a sign I need to "reboot" my neural network, my mind. It is a quick test or reminder that has survived over the years.

Usually, however, the reality is difficult and is not generous to offer me the kind of encouragement Mrs. Van Voorhis gave me. The challenging question still lingers: how can I enjoy learning and thinking when learning *how to learn and think* for the *instant I need it?*

The Real Challenge of Doing It Consistently

As a recap, I find that what makes learning or thinking fun is largely finding a process and the resultant reward of going through it. I also find that the process requires certain conditions, which are the wellness infrastructure support, a free explorative environment, and the drive to achieve and improve. Some of those famous geniuses had them more or less by accident, while other geniuses kept striving for them to reap the rewards of self-improvement in learning and thinking. It is true that even the great ones had good and bad moments of learning or thinking, as, for example, with areas of expertise and nonexpertise. But in their areas of expertise, they could turn bad moments into good moments. They knew how to do it on a dime.

At the beginning of this chapter I posed the question: if having fun was significant in learning and thinking, why and how did it really become useful, for instance, to the day-to-day reality of living? To answer that fully, I see that I first need to tackle the following question.

If those greats I listed above can do the learning or thinking very successfully, at *all* times—a lot easier, faster, deeper, and further than I just about any time, then is their level of proficiency something I can achieve? Especially if that is an acquired skill, then how can I train myself to get close to their level? After all, I *should be able* to discover *how* they actually attain proficiency for it, because it is another how-to question!

How Can I Always Be Able to Have Fun?

Without doubt, the word *fun* I is a relative term. Within the scope of learning and thinking, the specifics of fun vary from person to person. However, the fundamental sense of pleasure is common to all of us. It is the "I get it!" phenomenon with a brilliant *Aha!* elation. But it is inevitable that fun eventually faces a turn for a change. A discouraging feeling of uncertainty or loss of logic seeps in.

The previous chapter showed that in such a situation the technique to use is to focus on the question, "how can I get it?" That is to say, ask *how to find* the answer, not to *find* the answer. That is, it is now a question of process, a discovery process. When a discovery is made, it naturally leads to that "I get it" state. Thus the fun comes from going through the adventure of discovery and receiving its consequent reward. Achieving such a reward as understanding is especially satisfying because the process leading to it is truly a personal one yielding a sense of genuine achievement.

I start with an enthusiasm that I can discover the how-to process—how to learn or how to think, in ways similar to those great ones I described earlier. The reason for the enthusiasm is that the enthusiastic perspective is critical to knowing that in the long haul, I will find it. The intensity of my desire will make it possible. It is as if I really, *really* want to be a top chess master—if I want it so badly, I will eventually get it. Unfortunately, it may take some time, requiring extra energy and perseverance.

Toward accomplishing the challenge, I will now elucidate my thoughts, not specific steps. Why? Because I can then provide a higher-level view of what essential elements are involved in the process. In terms of the chess analogy, it is like asking what milestones I need to go through to become a chess master. Thus, I orient the direction of my thoughts toward a holistic view since I find that helpful as a breakthrough in my attempt. I will elaborate on what that means now.

First, I wish to recall the point about the three ingredients I identified previously for the process of learning or thinking. They are 1) being healthy, 2) being able to explore, and 3) being driven. The first is the supporting infrastructure. The second is execution. The third is energy. For the sake of discussion, I suppose all these three ingredients can be set aside as available.

To probe further what is really involved and seek the underlying principle, I now would like to look at a high-level picture first and then make a deep dive later.

The Big Picture

When I realize how I was able to study on the New York City subway feeling as if I were sitting on the dock at Deer Island of Upper Saranac Lake in serenity, I begin to think about the mental capability of the brain. When I become disciplined enough to be able to think about my mathematical problems from the night before immediately upon waking up, I begin to think about the physical capability of my whole body. When I realize I can set my feelings aside to go back to thinking, I begin to think about the emotional control I can develop. And when I realize my enthusiasm and positivity have a lot to do with the way I perform in athletics, I begin to think about the amazing effect that attitude can have on thinking. Simply put, I say the mind and body have so much influence on each other. That is, I can view how my mind functions from a physiological viewpoint. A physiological coordination is taking place when I think. My will can get me to act and perform extraordinary things, including even the act of thinking itself deep inside the brain!

Traditionally the mind and body are considered "distinct." The feelings belong to the heart, which is "separate" from the mind. But my point of the big picture is that it is all in my body. Just as I saw how my mental, physical, emotional, and neural facilities coordinate in my organic body, I would like to view my learning or thinking activities as a combined work in my organic being. The intent is not so much to distinguish mind matters from body matters as to highlight a holistic nature of work that is going on inside me. Why do I think that might be significant or beneficial for learning or thinking?

By viewing the activities in that light, I believe I can explain my theme better about how I might be able to achieve proficiency in learning and thinking. Elucidating the situations will lead to insightful paths for further exploration. And that in turn will yield more knowledge.

By now it is clearly no secret that I get excited about discussing my view—how I learn or think can be viewed physiologically as well as mentally. There are a number of key elements involved in my theme. I will introduce them to explain the theme simply but not in a precisely placed order, such as in academic papers.

The Elements

Words and Their Links

I first note that my learning or thinking uses words. Words are the building units for such an activity, just like the one or zero used in the computer as a base. I have learned many words over time through various experiences. I can recall the words as impressions of an experience. If I look inside myself, neurons in my brain and throughout the rest of my body are conducting signals supposedly to carry on such recalling activities.

When I experience or receive an impression, I can associate that with a set of words I know. I can explain it in associated words. So that means I have associations among the words. I will call such an association a link. Linking words can be based on a certain set of experiences or logic. If I encounter an unknown word, I try to link it to other words that I already know. That is to say, I search for links. Usually I do that when I try to explain something. I take it that those neurons have a lot to do with linking and searching.

If a set of links is found in such a situation involving an unknown search, I call that learning. If I chain the words using the set of links I just found, then the result is a description of an idea. Sometimes I simply ask a series of questions to seek a link for unknowns. That basically is thinking. In particular they respond to my questions, such as who, what, when, where, how, and why, to search for links that associate words. Evidently the neurons and their transmitters are known to perform such interactive work at blinding speed.

Because neurons and neurotransmitters in the neural network are said to be the media through which those activities take place, I can tie how successful I may become to the wellness of those physiological entities in my body.

Searches

When I learn or think, then I am looking for links, as in, "What does this concept of the Coriolis effect mean? Oh, yes, that means the earth's rotation impacts how the motion is perceived by an observer, depending on whether he is moving with the earth or not." Specifically, such guiding links can be a how-to link. In looking for links, certain associations help me with my search. Some associations are formed by memory links of past experiences, while others are formed by a set of guiding criteria, such as ethical values. Manuel's criterion to focus not on more profit but on more value to the customer is an example.

Thus, finding a how-to can lead to a discovery of links for words with a criteria control for that discovery. I apply such controls over how and where the search can occur, like a traffic control of signals for neurons over the neural network. That implies I deploy controls in terms of "words of reasons" to specify, for example, why the traffic can or cannot flow. When a link is finally established, I have a path and its reasons for the selection of the path. If it is a new path, I have learned something and expanded my neural network.

Character

Thus, the searches are controlled by criteria for a path selection. As I grow older, I accumulate my set of criteria. The cumulative formation over time becomes part of my character. It is comprised of guiding values, standards, and other criteria for selecting paths that link words and ideas. Among the factors that can impact the formation of my character is the culture I live in. For instance, an experience I gain while living in the culture generates certain expectations according to the culture and my character. Resulting deviations I observe from my original expectations will eventually help me identify my aspirations. Consequently my drive may grow stronger. That implies that a stronger energy can flow into my neural network and its infrastructure.

Organic Entities

As was already mentioned, all these can be looked at as an organic unit and the activities that support it. Words are impressions registered in my brain as units of expression. Paths link them for relays. When an event occurs, reactions call for a relayed action with certain reflexes or criteria. In describing the experience, I look for a path that will help me express it in words. If it is an unknown path without any criteria, a search ensues. The resulting experience leaves an impression in the neural network as an addition to the overall growth of the network. Naturally, the base structure for such growth is founded on the wellness of the organic entity. For neurons and neurotransmitters in the neural network, the wellness of the body matters because it secures the rapid information flow among them. For disciplines needed for sound path selection, the character of the person probably influences them most.

Integration

If I imagine all these pieces in a "summed diagram" of coordinated orchestration, I can begin to recognize a cycle or process having the following stages:

- I observe and describe events I experience in words, ask questions to link unknowns, confirm desired reasons for path selection, discover a set of paths, and review the learning I just experienced for the future.

- My neural network performs the messaging work. My character provides controls needed for the successful execution of learning and thinking. Finally I receive rewards, an enhancement to my organic entities. They include words, links, ideas, logic, and a self-generating learning capacity called intelligence.

Genius

Now, if a person working out these activities can outperform the "upper spectrum" of the norm in a specialized area in terms of such dimensions as the level of content, speed, distance, size, enumeration, and routes in the neural network, then I call such a person a genius. Normally they have a jump-start, as in a privileged youth or those with disciplined and accelerated growth. The jump-start sets a stage for the emergence of a genius. When I think of those greats mentioned earlier, I might want to characterize all of them as geniuses. Their achievements are exceptionally rare.

Could I train my organic entities to be like theirs, in a manner similar to those Olympic athletes who seek to attain their supreme level? Is it something attainable or trainable at all? Or can I emulate such a feat simply through an extreme desire to achieve my dream?

I see a possibility in working to raise the level of my goal. For if I set the highest goal I can ever set and feel truly and madly genuine about it, I could imagine myself getting all fired up to drive hard for it.

I almost accomplished such a feat when I set my goal high to pass my written qualifying examination for my doctoral program. I passed it with flying colors. My advisor, the late Cyrus Derman, and his colleague, the late Morton Klein, congratulated me on my "doing so well that only one before you might have done just as well in the department history."

But I also see that normally I will not get that motivated. As an ordinary human, I am mostly lazy. Hence one challenge is to discover how to motivate myself to a rare level (remember Buddha?). My experiences tell me that only after a disaster or encounter with the grandest inspiration to be part of the celebrated elite will I get an aspiration to do so. Otherwise it is hard work to get motivated on my own enough to form or bring out the big gun or a motivation rocket.

Clearly it is not attainable, at least normally, to reach the level of a genius quickly. (I say normally because there was a man who, after having been hit by a lightning, was able to play the piano like a phenomenal pianist![48]) But while attempting to reach such a genius level a step at a time, I can imagine training myself to improve my ability so I can discover how to learn or how to think. Depending on the intensity or my motivation, it might take a lifetime. But it is still reachable.

My big-picture perspective then is that I treat the challenge to discover the proficiency secret, by nature and by necessity, as a holistic one. By that I mean I would like to view everything that is involved in learning or thinking as a coordination of the human body in human living. My hope is that viewing the challenge from such a vista could yield a fresher or undiscovered thinking approach, generating excitement and enthusiasm.

---

48 *Daily Star* (Oneonta, NY), "Bolt leads to key moment," by Jake Palmateer, January 22, 2008, www.thedailystar.com/local/local_story_023040035.html. Also Oliver Sacks, *Musicophilia* (New York: Alfred A. Knopf, 2007), 3.

The Five-Step Approach

Based on the preceding explanation about my perspectives and the concept, I will now try to accommodate the first basic need. That is, I will provide the overall picture by elucidating a concrete approach regarding how to go about actually carrying out the process on demand.

As I mentioned earlier, for successful learning or thinking, three ingredients are essential to facilitate the process of how to do it. They are wellness, environment, and drive.

By applying my perspectives and the supporting concept to the challenge as described in terms of the elements above, I believe that the following steps below will help me. How will they help me? By raising the level of my performance in discovering the how-to, that is, by raising my performance of learning or thinking.

There are five action steps. They are for improving both *learning* and *thinking*:

1. **Observe**: details and processes, from different angles, levels, and culture

2. **Ask**: questions, with the first unknown impression encountered

3. **Confirm**: my goal and purpose, if it is high and genuinely motivating

4. **Discover**: paths, with imagination and discipline

5. **Review**: my performance and the process, as a routine habit

I would like to elaborate on each of the five action steps at this point.

First, as a preparatory note, here is a basic frame of reference from which the steps above should be viewed: learning or thinking is work that is *organic,* or *physiological.*

Thus, prior to going through the five steps, I need to be *feeling well enough* to undertake the challenge. The wellness of the neural network is critical to the cerebral engine. The fuel I need for it is my drive. Now I need to get my whole body ready for my cerebral activities—I should be able to say, *"Yes, I am able to start my engine!"*

The Observation

With all my senses in working shape, I try to catch *any* slight piece of information I receive or perceive; I dedicate all my energy to that at this point. My neural network is ready to sense anything, where the key medium of communication to my brain is words. The first step, therefore, is to cognize what I observe in terms of words. After the observation, I try to *explain* to myself what I just observed. The selection of the words is important:

Start elucidating with precise diction.

The Asking

I now start asking questions about what I elucidate. I fire up the neural engine in my neural network to seek links. The secret to the search is the form of the query, how to phrase it.

Keep my query short and simple.

For example, I start with the 5W1H interrogatives: who, what, when, where, why, and how. Then I try to force an answer to ask more questions about the results. They usually have connotations and implications for further querying:

- *Why*—for the goal, the purpose, or the criteria

- *How*—for the path selection on which how-to to use

- *What*—for the specifics of the detailed words

The Confirmation

Here I get a chance to feel honest about why I want to do what I am trying to do. The ultimate test of authenticity is to answer some hard questions, such as why does it matter? Why put myself through it? I need to be sure and determined for the neurons to perform their part; otherwise it is like trying to shoot the puck in a hockey game without being sure of where the goal is. My body cannot function as one unit to deliver results if I am not yet confirmed about my decision.

The neural signals need guidance with the direction of the flow in the network. Their journey to find links for the words that meet the goal is myopic without my firmness.

Is the destination my true target? Am I ready to fight off any distractions that might lie ahead?

The Discovery

Now my neural network is ready for action: I can aim clearly, get my mental coordination set, and fire the guns. Such an execution is controlled, in part, by the quality of my personal character, that is, the set of standards I follow and the values and criteria I uphold. If I think about the choices, there are so many paths of learning and thinking: useless paths, counterproductive paths, and even immoral paths. None of them may be appealing, and I go on discovering more new paths. It is not easy, but with creativity and imagination, the work may even turn into a pleasant challenge. With discipline I know the sense of hardship tends to disappear. Pain goes away with the intense mental focus of being charged up to do some learning or thinking. Many ancient Greeks used logic to guide thoughts; Descartes analyzed things piecemeal, logically. To Gauss, photographic memories of numbers would have been a joyful aid to learning. Thus, there does not seem to be one fixed approach to discovering the how to. Hence, in each instance, I seek paths that will help me discover the *process* of learning or thinking. Like those thought experiments that Albert Einstein performed in his brain, let the network expand in the universe of unknown paths.

Go for a neural adventure, and search for imaginative how-tos!

The Review

After my exploration it is time for me to reflect on my performance. I summon all my body elements to report the results, from the sense of satisfaction of my accomplishment to confidence in my understanding, for example. Any lessons I learn I feed back into my knowledge bank for a future encore with improvements. Organically I gain more experiences toward finding the *process* in terms of speed and strength for a path search, as well as registering the results for the neurotransmitters. The review adds quality and strength to my character. The overall cerebral faculty, commonly known as intelligence, grows.

Keep learning, and keep stimulating the neural network for a better discovery of how-tos!

As I mentioned, these five action steps arose as a result of integrating my perspectives with my concept about *learning* and *thinking*, or *how to learn* and *how to think*. The five-step approach seems fairly ordinary. To see the potential, I now would like to consider its practical viability. In particular, I carry it forward to test myself: will this help me learn or think more thoroughly?

How Would That Really Work for Me?

To answer the question, I can cite specific examples for each step:

1. **Observe—Am I missing anything?**

   Hint: Some things are staring right at me.

   This example is from many years ago when I was working for Trans World Airlines. A friend of mine, Steve, my colleague at TWA, came over one afternoon to chat with me about the exam he had to pass as part of work toward his master's in computer science at NYU. He remarked that he would do fine because he had done his best in preparing. But I cautioned him by saying that his "best" was based on what he saw, what he observed. He did not know what he did not know or what he was missing. He could not see some things that I saw. One example was a set of assumptions he had to use in his logic. He did not know that he could or should challenge a condition underlying some of the assumptions. Later I heeded that caution in my own efforts. Whenever I felt something was staring at me but I could not see it because I was not trained to see it, I challenged my best "gut-feel" search and began to look for different searches on a clean slate.

I am usually not that alert unless or until I remind myself to be so. Manuel was a keen observer because he was desperate to survive for his family. (When it was not a desperate situation, he was normal like me. One memorable experience was that he could hardly learn how to produce the *r* sound. I went over and over it with him by explaining what I had learned from Silas. But he could not care less about it, no matter how embarrassing it was to him!) When he sensed urgency, he turned on his keen observation switch instantly. He once confided to me that he observed intensely how a Chinese grocer across the street competed with him. He saw how the competitor matched or tried to outperform him by raising or lowering his prices, even copying his move to change the display locations of his merchandise from one day to the next. It was like a survival battle. If I were as intense with my observation as Manuel was with his grocery business, I probably would have done better in many cases. With what I could see, I could explain the nature of the challenge to myself more clearly. And that probably made me think differently and further. So the tip is to be physically, mentally, and emotionally alert!

2. **Ask—I can always ask "How?" or "Why?"**

Reminder: There is always that 5W1H to begin a question: *Who, What, When, Where, Why, and How.*

The interrogatives known as the 5W1H are so simple and yet so powerful.
A good example is to hear how a toddler asks questions, innocently but directly to nail the center of the issue. The child is not afraid to ask. There is no malicious intent, only straightforward queries. Asking a question is like extending a potential link or search path in the dark. Small steps make it easy to build paths.

When I realized that the rules of Romaji as an aid for pronunciation did not go well with English words, I could have asked, "Why, what is wrong?" I did not know they were not applicable to English words, especially how to pronounce them. I did not know that Romaji was intended for Westerners learning to pronounce Japanese words. But I never asked any questions!

Often I hear that questions are more important than the answers. Why? I see that questions tend to direct my thoughts, but because questions are not helping me link words yet (that is, no answers are formed yet) and are still mysterious to me, they facilitate my trying a new path. If the words in the question are repeated not as a question but as a statement, they tend to stir up mostly the existing ideas already linked to them, producing few new ideas. Words and ideas given in a statement are already connected, in effect, yielding a situation like being in a cul-de-sac with no outlet. That is some difference. Questions that challenge the given with respect to providing better elucidation and right diction can certainly help make that new connection happen. Simple questions are especially effective when the ideas are complex and can more easily help me reach my goal. In that regard, I wish I had attained the ability to pose simple questions more freely, especially earlier in life. I really admire young children who can freely do that because they are developing the query function with their neural network!

3. **Confirm—Am I sure this is really, truly what I want?**

Hint: Thoughts are tied to the goal.

In searching for paths, it would be a lot easier if I knew the destination than if I did not. That I know based on my experience, learned in a harsh manner. Along the way I gradually learned to confirm whether my destination was reasonable. In a way it is like letting my ambition illuminate my goal area like a lighthouse. The further I aim, the further I feel I could advance. I need to point my search in the right direction by confirming that it is really where I want to go. As shown in my experience below, not having a clear and definitive aim can lead to a disaster.

I once made my great uncle, John K. Inadomi, the elder brother of Manuel Inadomi, and John's wife, Mitsuyo, very angry. In December of 1965, they gave me $250 or so as part of their aid to my school expenses at South Kent. Did I spend it wisely? Not really. I spent it on a plane ticket to Pompano Beach, Florida, because my roommate, Jim Denham, invited me for Christmas. I justified it on the basis that it was part of my education, some extracurricular activities. Well, it did not go well. To the Inadomis, it sounded like I wanted a vacation. To me, that notion did not really enter my mind. My goal was not vacation but learning. Aunt Mitsuyo wrote me a long letter chiding me that the money was given to me in memory of my grandmother (she was a sister of John Inadomi), and it was never meant to subsidize a vacation. I apologized to her profusely. My parents apologized to her profusely, too. I thought they would condemn me for it. But in retrospect I did not think much of it really.

Why? Because, believe or not, I did the same thing the following winter—only I took a train rather than a plane! It was like I did it in defiance of great aunt Mitsuyo with some sort of a message that I did not think it was that bad.

Manuel thought I was still young. He did not say I was a fool, just young. When I think about that experience now, I feel I could have done better. I thought I did think about my decision carefully then. But I could have been smoother by first asking Mitsuyo for her approval (I knew I had a good case for it). I could have been more sensitive to her because she and her husband had left Japan almost penniless and headed for California to be farm laborers (like Manuel), but they saved every penny they earned to build a successful chain of supermarkets, not just once but twice (they lost all the first stores due to World War II internment but repeated the feat from scratch all over again after the war). I could have thought many other things, I suppose. I did not know that I was not thinking thoroughly even though I felt I was more mature than most in my age group. I definitely could have thought more deeply by asking myself the question of "why do I want it?" genuinely and sharing it with her with enthusiasm.

I judged that my thoughts were viable because they would help me achieve my goal. I certainly should have confirmed that!

4. **Discover—I am free to be as creative and imaginative as I want to be.**

Hint: This is the crux of the thinking activity.

The next step involves asking how to get to the destination from where I start. Do I use the path of my past experience and knowledge? But how would I know if it is a good one? In choosing a path, I am revealing the criterion that I used to make the choice. One practical way to get started is to just choose any starting path and see where it takes me—hopefully not too far off from the one leading to the goal. I could also try shifting my viewpoint, challenging authority, reversing the time frame, expunging the status quo, changing the given scenarios, etc. The neurons looking for links need help. The source of their energy is the gusto of curiosity, not grueling pressure to find paths. I am the controller: I keep my goal in mind; I choose my paths.

Here is an example of a problem with which I had no previous experience. Remember my first year in Columbus, Indiana? I had lived in Manhattan for a long time, and now I was standing in the middle of a cornfield in Indiana, trying to find some entertainment for a weekend. I had already asked myself the "why" question—why I was there in the cornfield and not in Manhattan. That helped me set my goal. OK, I was now a transplant Hoosier. I needed to start living there and enjoying it, I told myself. So I gathered some facts about the town. I saw some sites with architecture, nature, and the towns nearby with a lot of history. Next I tried using criteria for path selection. The one of trial and error was painfully time-consuming. I talked to my landlady. She was no help: having come from Ukraine, she wanted to know that herself! I tried my boss and colleagues of my age group. They finally had a lot of suggestions and even invitations! Again my destination was not to find a specific thing to do for that weekend; my true destination was to find a *process* for determining a specific thing to do for that weekend *and* future weekend. Thus, I found it—I found a successful path of gut and experience: check things out with those with the knowledge —your friends!

In science and technical areas, it may be easier because I can build, however minutely, a path stepwise on previous steps that I learned using numbers and experiments. It is not difficult to apply that same principle to things like, for example, Microsoft Excel or any other computer software. The path to discovery of how to learn such subjects is to build block upon block with diligence.

In other areas things are usually not that simple. Say I am given a responsibility to hire an employee. I do the preparation work regarding the job description and the type of candidate I am looking for. Suppose I have half a dozen candidates. How can I select my how-to approach? How should I think about the selection process? In the final decision point, I end up doing authentically whatever comes closest to my goal. Often I use an approach that relies on my common sense. Sincerity, for example, can be sighted in the candidate's manner of speech, as it reflects the person's thinking process and reaction behavior. The key is keeping my goal in mind: a search for the "best match" candidate. And I want to do that genuinely, free from any

pressure to impress others or distraction generated by other "selfish" goals.

When I first started to work for Manuel, I was
given a cashier's job. I had to ring up sold merchandise in his liquor store, return change to
the customer promptly and accurately, watch for
theft, and balance the book at the end of my shift.
I was reluctant to get started. But he told me to
just start doing it with a trainer standing next
to me—a case of jump right in, less "theoretical
talk." To my surprise, I learned fast. So to this day,
jumping right in is a good how-to I often use when
my goal is to get experience right away. I feel I am
training those neurons by fire, fast and effectively.

In academic search work, the hardship is somewhat greater because often it is all in my head: no
coins, no merchandise, and no people. The selection of a how-to can get a bit easier with the use of
logical criteria, such as definitions, testing of hy-
potheses, and rhetorical argument. As I take more
interest, I find it easier to retain the key ideas in
my head, linking them in some ways step-by-step.
So in a way, the difficulty is a symptom of lacking
genuine desire, as in misguided goal-seeking actions. Somehow the neurons are not cooperating
because they face "subtle" resistance!

Whether or not I have a genuine desire is a test of
character. And that brings up the very important
final step.

5. **Review—Do I want to learn or think better next time or not?**

Hint: This is the crux of learning activity.

The final step helps me with the real test: do I really care about my performance, how well I learned or thought?

The hard part is that all these thinking activities take place on the cerebral level. If I feel I did not think very smartly in one instance, I do not want to repeat the same thinking approach. On the other hand, if I did think well, I want to repeat it. The desire here is cerebral. If I am really, *really* hungry for it, I will review my performance to improve it. However, such a desperate hunger is normally absent, and instead, I know and realize I should improve my performance, because I feel there is some pressure or expectation from someone *else* that I am supposed to do better. The motivation is not *my* desire to achieve my goal, but to satisfy someone else's needs. That is where my character can step in to get me back on the right track.

If I could see how the neurons were being deployed to achieve the task of reviewing and assessing my performance by tracing the paths of my thoughts, I might find they possess varying levels of energy. My desperation, hunger, enthusiasm, and optimism might contribute to an excited state. Or the discipline power in my character may be forcing the neural signals to move reluctantly, for example, to control anger involving incorrect assumptions. So in whatever state they are in, or regardless of what causes the neurons to get busy, they could get into a routine mode, contributing to the growth of my neural network's infrastructure accordingly. That implies the growth is influenced by how motivated I am to improve my own character. So the reviewing step helps me with a reminder to improve my control of my character in order to improve my learning or thinking.

Here is an example from the time I spent with the Dietels. It is somewhat lengthy, but the rationale is that the lengthy description will provide a more accurate picture.

I used to tell myself never to say I was tired because I knew the second I said that, I would become tired and unable to think. My reasoning was, "If I think I am tired and tell myself that, then I am tired." I refused to acknowledge it. That was when I was up till 3:00 a.m. and got up at 6:00 a.m. while living with the Dietels. I would go jogging first thing around the Emma Willard campus to wake myself up. I first thought it was a kind of silly thing as there really was nobody running in those days. But I repeated it. Every morning as I got up, I kept saying, "No, I am not really tired yet." I also trained myself to start thinking right away once my eyes were open. At first it was a bit of a struggle. But I found a way.

I got into the habit of leaving a set of notes and books on a desktop the night before. As soon as I got up, I recalled the mental status of the night before when I had prepared them, and I was able to link up my neurons in the network. I did that routine of three hours of sleep a night for about three months, and I got good grades, including an A in German. But naturally my body started to break down. I became ill. Linda began to worry about me, so she arranged an international call to enable my parents to call and talk to me. Bless her heart; I felt so touched by her thoughtfulness. It was my sophomore year at Rensselaer. I had not talked to my folks since I'd left Japan four years before. International calls back then, in 1968, were very expensive and normally had to go through an operator.

Years later Bill asked me several times how I managed that schedule. I myself wonder today how I got so motivated to withstand such a punishing routine. I learned how to study by the force of discipline. But where did that force come from? It came from my strong sense of a goal, and I reviewed my performance constantly against that goal. I attribute such an effort to my discipline, to my character. In a somewhat circular logic, my character did grow by such a daily review. I was desperate to achieve my goal.

What kind of goal did I have? I had a single goal: to get a college education in the United States. I had no financial means, so my scholarship was my only source of income. I was able to live with the Dietels, which meant as long as I did my required chores, I was able to live for free. But to keep up the scholarship, I had to maintain a B average. So doing my academic work successfully was the key to my continuing to live in the United States. Given that goal and the determination to achieve it, the physical pain was easy to take.

In subjects like German, although it was very foreign to me at first, it became easier and easier to advance; it was almost a repeat of learning English. (Bill evidently called the Dean of Rensselaer to question why students like me had to learn German while still struggling with English!) Organic chemistry was a near disaster because I had no idea how to learn those terms and handle lab results (I could hardly understand the instructions, let alone write a report!) So that is why I feel that neurons cooperate according to how my character feels about the subject.

I had to have strong discipline, but that was a natural consequence of my determination. I had a lot of temptations, especially living on the campus of the girls' preparatory school, Emma Willard, or just having fun with the Dietel kids, taking them for rides in my 1962 Ford Galaxy convertible (it was such a spectacular experience to floor it through a carpet of fallen leaves on a crisp fall day to get a feel of a V-8 response!). But my character was strong enough to resist overindulging in temptations during the first year because I knew that nourishing my character was my top priority to ensure I would not derail from my path of learning. The strong sense of purpose, why I wanted to succeed, was always there. That is why I feel I could probably achieve a similar feat today, given a strong desire to continue to grow and a healthy body to put my neurons in a row!

These are my explanations to support my claim that the above five-step approach would help me learn or think better. The true test is how the approach would work in the real world...... and can that be fun and easy?

Again, here is a summary of the five steps in a nutshell:

Motivate the body and the psyche. Provide ample time to start sending signals to those neurons in the neural network. Then, to learn or think successfully, keep the following steps in mind:

1. Observe details, as in "What on earth do I have here?" Let neurons carry the messages freely.

2. Ask simple and brief questions to force easy answers. Start firing up neurons to determine easy paths.

3. Confirm goals and purposes, as in, "Why on earth do I want this?" Identify the furthest targets as the final destinations of the paths.

4. Discover reasons and criteria for paths, as in "How on earth can I get there?" Be creative in selecting specific paths.

5. Review your performance for growth, as in "I want to keep learning!" Remember the search history, and learn from it to enhance the quality of your character.

My bold claim, as I implied before, is that if I find learning or thinking not easy or not much fun, then I need to go through the steps because my efficiency is low. If I follow the above five steps, I say I will be able to find a high-efficiency how-to approach for more thorough thinking!

Will It Really Work for Me in the Real World?

Now that I have elaborated how to use the steps, it is time to expand and consider some actual cases and demonstrate how the steps can benefit me in the real world.

Examples from the Business World

There are two examples from the business world. I am familiar with both of them as part of my profession spanning nearly half a century. The first deals with a company decision to outsource a set of functions. The second one challenges the validity of common practices in evaluating employee performance.

I worked in the airline industry for over a quarter of a century, four years at Trans World Airlines and twenty-four years at United

Airlines. My jobs were mostly technical, consultative, and administrative. I saw change agents impacting the industry, such as deregulation, an employee stock ownership program, bankruptcy, and outsourcing. The ups and downs reminded me of my personal ups and downs. Two experiences in particular became so relevant to me because of the ideas in my theme. One is a case of outsourcing, the other a case of the management performance review process. The essential question was, if I were to go through them as a "decision maker" on how they should be handled, would I be able to think well? If I were to apply my approach to those cases, would I be a better thinker?

Naturally, real-world situations are far more complex than meets the eye. The scope is far wider. Revisiting the past may not be productive in general because it is easy to be critical in retrospect without presenting substantial proof today. Despite such a shortcoming, I hope this discussion will be of use. I will stay focused on the issue of how to achieve successful learning and thinking.

Outsourcing Decision Making

The first point to note here again is that reality is just full of constraints, which come in variety: business world priorities, political pressures, time pressures, and limits of competence and imagination of those who work, to name a few. Expectedly they complicate thinking.

The question is whether or not the workers in such a reality can think successfully, specifically by the approach discussed above. We will stay on that main issue rather than the surrounding ones, such as how to meet the challenge of convincing or communicating successfully to those who are in decision-making positions. So now I will go through a good thinking session and have some fun along these lines.

A company decides to outsource its benefits department. The department has administered health and pension benefits for its employees and retirees up to that point. In evaluating the benefits of outsourcing, the decision makers rely on a consulting firm, which is paid by them to do a quick study of the situation. The consultants come up with their recommendation, which, not surprisingly, goes along with the management's preference. The preference is driven by the then-fashionable idea of eliminating functions that are not part of the core business to achieve lower labor costs, that is, outsourcing. The prospect of instant cost savings propels the company to proceed quickly.

The end result, however, turns out to be a disaster due to a noticeable deterioration in service quality and employee morale. The decision makers in the top management begin to wonder what went wrong. Typical situations included slow and inaccurate administration of benefits, additional work to correct mistakes (which involves twice the effort, first to undo the initial work and then to do it correctly), and rapidly increasing customer complaints . I was managing a small group of analysts, partially supporting top administrators with computer reports and analyses, so I saw the impact firsthand. That is why I selected this case. My question here is whether or not the senior management would have found the five-step approach useful and whether it might have led them to a different decision.

To set a common playing field, here are the background conditions:

The company is facing a possible near-term bankruptcy.

The decision of who is to receive the outsource contract is up to a director of the benefits department. (Here, according to the director, the fundamental decision of whether to outsource or not had, effectively or in actuality, been made by the director's bosses as a foregone conclusion. It is a good example of a contradictory but common phenomenon in the constrained reality.) The scope and definition of outsourcing is not fully defined because the job is being rushed. The statement of work requirements created for the potential vendors does not address many of the details.

There is a popular trend of outsourcing as a solution to reduce costs in the US business world.

The business of the company, in case a reminder is necessary, is in transportation (airline) industry.

The benefits department consists of about fifty employees in "full-time equivalence," consisting of fifteen management workers, and forty-five clerical workers, both full- and part-time. They perform all benefits administration work under highly complex policies in a fairly efficient manner. There are few complaints about inaccuracies and little tardiness in processing claims.

The corporate information technology (IT) division and my small group in human resources (HR) division support the automated processing tasks, with high degrees of cooperation and coordination.

The challenge is for the director of the benefits department to decide quickly to whom she should outsource her department function. (Again she was evidently "told" to outsource by her higher-ups.) Naturally she had to act fast, so she could not have thought about the decision thoroughly. Would she have benefited from the five-step approach, and if so, how and to what extent?

The director made a quick decision (within three months) to outsource to an outfit that was new to the benefits administration profession. The conversion to the outfit was done quickly, in about a year. Her rationale was cost savings. After the switch, the quality of service deteriorated rapidly and steeply, with frequent breakdowns of the computerized system. It became evident that the vendor the department outsourced to could handle neither the complexity nor the volume of work. The extra work in the computer programming and retroactive correction and updating tasks that followed created huge problems for IT. The customers, that is, the employees and retirees, who expected continued good service, began to file complaints about the frequent delays and incorrect payments for the claims submitted.

The common notion is that it is not a good idea to put a price tag on immeasurable entities, such as thoughtful services delivered by human resources personnel and the value of human motivations. And yet the normal manner of operation is to justify the management actions in terms of dollars and cents. The goals are usually driven by the dominant forces of corporate culture, that is, higher profit and lower cost. The benefits department director was clearly under the gun by her superiors with tremendous pressure to produce results and reduce costs quickly. As promised earlier, rather than criticizing her decision in retrospect, I would like to stay focused on the effectiveness of the five-step approach.

The framework of the approach is to observe as much as possible sharply and ask simply with the interrogatives such as how, why, and what. It also includes confirming and keeping our goal in mind, as well as discovering how to go about selecting our thinking approach.

Now in terms of the five steps, it is reasonable to suppose the following constraining scenarios she had to operate under:

The observation: everything is for cost reduction mandated by the top management.
The department is not necessarily a core business function.
The corporation needs to cut costs wherever possible, very quickly; they need to show the results to the shareholders and the Wall Street analysts, fast.

The inquiry: how can such a cost reduction be achieved quickly?
Why does the corporation have such a department?
Where can it cut costs quickly, as it is already loosing a lot of money?
Why not outsource it?

The confirmation of purpose:
The first priority is for the corporation to show the results of cost-cutting efforts quickly.
Find and go with the lowest bidder unless it's obvious it won't work.
Minimize cost by doing work with the least staff.
Realize the gain as soon as possible by laying off workers within three months of the cutover.

The discovery of the approach for thinking:
Go along with the senior management.
Conduct fast cost benefit analysis with consultants confidentially, without staff involvement (as layoff information should not be shared with them).
Review vendors' capabilities quickly with a brief request for proposal (RFP).

Here is a real-world translation of these in plainer English. The goal is set for her. The people at the top of the corporation are telling her to do certain things for the company; she is expected to find a justification for the actions that sounds politically correct, even though she knows it does not seem right. But the company is not a democratic institution; she needs to obey the order.

As for the discovery step, there is the time constraint, which means it is nearly impossible to do the right thing; just imagine asking Thomas Jefferson to draft the Declaration of Independence in several hours! Such a constraint could create an environment where sloppy "fudge" work in the financial books is allowed to be used to substantiate an improvement in the bottom line of the company.

So how should I think here if I were responsible for the decision making? I could go through the steps.

One scenario is to force top management to display all the cards on the table. Imagine how Warren Buffett or Peter Drucker would elucidate possibilities and their consequences clearly and rigorously.

In particular, more discussions could elaborate on such topics as the objectives, the scope of outsourcing, and the method of vendor selection. The specific purpose of the management, to cut costs quickly, was not really one of greatness, as they were trying to win a small battle and not the war. Manuel might have challenged the wisdom to focus so much on expenses, especially due to the minute amount of savings in relation to the large "cost" due to loss of employee trust and goodwill.

On the technology side, except for those who dealt with the operation, few in top management really had knowledge of the complexity and scope of the logic used in the processing of benefits information.

To provide a feel for the extent of the logic, I have collected the essential factors involved in the appendix. The unfortunate fact was that the knowledge was not fully documented by the experts. There simply were not enough resources to do the documentation work. Also, the standard paperwork, like requests for proposals, could not have captured the depth without the experts. From that view the projected savings were based practically on fictions of an ideal world. Few vendors could handle the complex benefits administration work specific to the transportation industry. With huge numbers of labor union rules and complex exceptions and revisions negotiated over decades, benefit rules evolved into something very hard to document.

In short, the decision-making task needed far more thinking than ordinary, but the reality made it almost impossible to do. It was, in a way, doomed to fail. Who is responsible for that? Putting on a Manuel Inadomi hat, I would say it is the top management. They constrained the thinking capacity of the organization. In my opinion, the director was neither incompetent nor derelict in her duties. So most likely I will be accurate in holding the senior management responsible for the ineffective business strategy.

Going back to the five steps, I, as the decision maker, could have done more thorough thinking using the approach. But because the senior management had already decided on the effort, I could not have altered the course. A corporation is different from an individual, in that a corporation works as a hierarchical unit. It apparently cannot think like a person as it needs to execute an order. Hence the five-step approach has a limitation and needs to be modified accordingly. It could be the subject of a future essay! In the meantime my hope is that the approach, at the least, will help thinking and learning wherever applicable. I believe *I* will be better off applying the approach even in a corporate world. The fifth step, the review step, helps me realize the limit of what I could do in a corporation, but at the same time it highlights the great, constant need to improve my own capability in thinking and learning.

I now turn to my second example. It is a case of an employee performance evaluation task in business. This is based on my experience as well.

Performance Evaluation Task

As most of you are aware, a performance evaluation in business is a review of how an employee performed for her (or his) organization. The intention is basically good. Occasionally, however, it gets a little wacky for several reasons. For instance, it tries to condense all the verbal reviews into numbers for comparison purposes with her peers to compute her merit increases or decreases. Secondly the objectivity expressed in numbers is often lost or overruled by political maneuvers and economic forces, such as reduction in force or layoffs. The end result, more often than not, is that it loses the purpose and effectiveness—it's not an accurate evaluation. Furthermore, sometimes it is unnecessarily dispiriting to the employee because, more often than not, it is rather counterproductive. In my view it should be done differently.

First, chances are that it's hard to convert into numbers the employee's skills, abilities, and performance, like business acumen, innovation, and teamwork. How accurately and justifiably can a person's contributions to her group of colleagues be "evaluated" and then described by numbers? Discussions, instead, should be carried out continuously throughout the year with the

131

employee to effectively assess, among other things, the quality of her work, skills, abilities, and her contribution to her organization. The reviewer should know the facts and communicate the resulting assessment for mutual understanding genuinely and conscientiously.

Critical observations aside, however, it is fair to acknowledge that a lot of work is done in this area professionally, such as in the fields of psychology and organization effectiveness. For that reason, I would like to limit our scope to how to think better for conducting a performance review more successfully.

Confirming the Purpose

The purpose of the thinking here (or the "why" of it), from the viewpoint of ensuring the highest goal, is to discover how best to communicate certain basic messages, such as what the employer wants the employee to do more of or less of.

Depending on the scope and definition of performance, the reviewer may wish to target different goals. The goals can be a list of accomplishments specific to projects underway. It may include developmental pieces, like assertiveness skills. It may be a tool used for merit increase (or decrease) determination. For a list of accomplishments, it is necessary to think about how to track and communicate that accurately. On the other hand, if it is for merit increase calculation, it would be a good idea to expand the goal of the thinking further to communicate such information as the industry norm, market conditions, etc. In hard times, a mere 2 percent increase in pay might be a great achievement. In any event, the critical step is to clearly define the purpose of the thinking task: what is the purpose of the performance review?

Discovering the Approach

Next, given the purpose above, the approach (or the how-to) needs to be addressed, such as, how can I actually and effectively think to help attain that goal? It also needs to be communicated openly. To enable such a communication task, for example, one approach is to consider doing research on communication techniques that already exist in the market. Or consider asking the employees via surveys how they wish to be evaluated in performance. Other approaches might be to check out technologies that are already available to facilitate the process. Or, in the face of difficulty of ensuring the integrity and objectivity of the evaluation, a logistically simpler and less expensive evaluation may be considered. Regardless, there are a lot of thinking approaches to attain the given goal.

Reviewing the Outcome

The actual work is to search for answers to the above questions, or think about the "what." Today there are many ways to get an employee's information on tasks accomplished through the Internet, such as Twitter and blogging. Likewise, evaluation techniques must be available very easily. Beyond what's practiced, it is always possible to think of creative methods that are win-win cases for both reviewer and employee. The employee could be responsible for his or her self-assessment, given enough information about the task. The employee might naturally be able to suggest improvements to company operations or strategies, which could improve the bottom line. It may turn out irrelevant or ineffective to associate the performance with some numerical scaling or do the "normalization" for merit increases, however. After all, what are the real differences between a high-performing employee and a low-performing employee? Often it is relative, subjective, and rather unstable in the judgment. Overall corporate or business climate or trends may color the performance picture viewed by the reviewer. In an ideal case, employees tend to perform well regardless of a performance evaluation or merit increase if their sense of mission is made clear to them—that the most relevant value for them is being valuable to the organization. And that is certainly relative, subjective, or personal as well. Thinking and coming up with answers along these lines is surely challenging. But the good news is there are many, many good questions and ideas that will help improve the review process! When that spirit of cooperative improvement is sensed, it is a less resentful experience.

I picked these examples from the business world because they are somewhat easier to follow—after all, they are real cases. My point here is that things done in business can be imperfect in most cases, but with clear thinking, I have huge faith that they will be improved a great deal, and very quickly, once the leaders at the highest levels recognize they could do better. The rationale is that it is our human nature; there is always someone in business who wants to do better in the capitalistic sense than the "others." All in all, I believe it was fun to think about these real examples.

Back to the earlier question of use: if having fun is significant in learning and thinking, why and how did it really become useful, for instance, in the day-to-day reality of living? The answer hinges on my developing the ability to discover the how-tos when necessary. It is clear it is useful. But doing it once is easy (perhaps); it is a lot harder to do it on a consistent basis. That, then, implies the tougher questions: Will I ever attain the proficiency of discovering how to think well in my lifetime if not in a short time period? Will I ever be able to deliver a great performance every time in a consistent manner?

I remain optimistic about that because I know how to do it. It will depend on having a healthy body first, a friendly environment second, and third, a strong hunger for self-improvement. It will depend on how well I perform the iterative process of observing, querying, confirming, discovering, and reviewing for learning and thinking. If I am fortunate, I should be able to enjoy the fruit of such an effort to explore new worlds of ideas and knowledge. It is work, but it is *fun* work because I know I will enjoy the resulting reward.

A part of such fun comes in the form of an opportunity to dream. I feel highly enthusiastic about the practicality and the applicability my approach provides. For example, I can move on to consider the implications and potentials of the ideas behind my approach. It seems I could push the limits further and further, and if that is what I am supposed to aim for in this life, what kind of life would it be after I became proficient? How would I contribute to the world and what would be my legacy?

I would like to at least peek at some of the potentials. I would like to start by revisiting some of the basic ideas and thoughts. For instance, what do we mean by having smart or stupid thoughts? Or, if I feel the five-step approach might indeed be a powerful panacea for human shortcomings such as bigotry and intolerance, I want to explain how that might help in fixing them. And if my thoughts are on a wrong path because some of my existing perceptions might be leading me astray, I want to highlight that and improve myself.

I have a feeling that through such exercises, I might be able to explore the boundaries of human possibilities in thinking. After I truly learn the words and ideas that have built today's world, I could continue to produce new ones, and at the same time, I could recall those paths that would help predict consequences, or equivalently, find "answers" to my questions, each and all—wait, do I imply *all* the questions and their answers? Most likely not in the near term. But will it be truly possible to come close to achieving such a state? What kind of frontier it will be, I am curious to know.

Well, shall we begin a journey to frontiers and beyond?

Exploring for
More Fun

Now it is time to have *real fun*—explore and discover the how-tos and their hidden potentials. What might be a good warm-up exercise to begin the journey of exploring the potentials? The excitement here is that there will be something of value in the pursuit of unknowns and mystery because, for example, prejudice, bigotry, and narrow-mindedness should be cured with or without travel.[49] Let us see if we can think to find solutions to some of the challenging situations in our universe!

I will consider a case of an elderly person with some symptoms of dementia, which is said to cause loss of such abilities as cognition and reasoning. That is, learning or thinking activities seem to be the main target of the disease. Many medical advances have been made, and yet no cure for dementia has been found. Some even suggest music as an effective therapy. That is an interesting point: why music? If music is a representation of a person's feelings or

---

49 "Travel is fatal to prejudice, bigotry and narrow-mindedness, and many of our people need it sorely on these accounts," [Mark Twain, *Innocents Abroad* (Kindle Edition, 1869 First Edition), 364.]

expressive cognition of a reality, then there must be some commonality or relevance; certain melodies may help recall associated memories or thoughts.

To explain it from the perspectives of the last chapter, I note the following areas of work for the elderly to become aware of first:

- **Body**—Get active physically (be healthy).
- **Attention**—Get a structure to apply some discipline to (wake up; shake up).
- **Neurals**—Do a recall exercise for paths (words, ideas) by curiosity (observe, ask, confirm, discover) and avoid temptations (fun without work).
- **Coordination**—Integrate paths in the network with your character (review; generate hunger).

Suppose an elderly woman has stopped working on some of the routine steps. And suppose music therapy is given to her. With music therapy, associations might be reestablished among her neurons. For instance, if a short piece by Vivaldi or Mozart is played, some of the harmonious and creative melodies could trigger and reactivate old paths in her brain that are associated with apt moods and imaginations. She might find an old road back to the area she used to play in, which might help her recall forgotten memories. At least it sounds like a plausible thought to try to explain the effect of music therapy on dementia in the elderly.

The above is an example of how the five-step perspectives could explain conditions involving mental "disorder." Furthermore, some of the common conditions might be dealt with through an exercise of the five steps. What I would like to do next is to extend such a line of thinking to explain other ideas, only with a bit more elucidation. As my discussion is by no means academic, I take the liberty of pacing it loosely and casually. To me that is both fun and exciting because then I can extend my learning or thinking capacity even further!

Explaining a Few Things from the Perspectives

As related above in the discussion on dementia in the elderly, the perspectives involve the following three areas: the infrastructure of the neural network, execution of a search for paths linking words, and the energy to drive and grow. I am implying such a viewpoint is helpful in explaining some of the well-known, fundamental principles.

Before I go further, I post a word of caution! Although I begin with real "basic" fundamentals, my discussion can get rather "deep" very quickly. Because it is an exploration, paths could get lost very easily. It will probably lack thrills because it is not you but *I* who lead the exploring; it is like trying to find gold without 100 percent of your freedom to explore. So expand your imagination and join me on my ride.

We now begin, starting with the fundamentals.

Equivalent Being: As Descartes stated, most of us (excluding those unfortunate folks born with mental defects) are essentially equal with respect to having functioning, healthy minds and bodies. That equitable condition can be expressed in terms of having essentially a normal functioning number of neurons and neurotransmitters in the neural network. The definition of equality can therefore be dealt with physiologically.

The Neural Network: The neural network develops a mechanism to use words in the language as a basic unit of acknowledgment or cognition. Specifically, the mechanism includes linking and registering the words in the brain, associated with the experiences one goes through. The linked words can form an associated content or an idea. Such registering is said to be performed partly by the messengers known as neurotransmitters. As with any growth, the more their signals traverse through the network, the greater their performance becomes. The organic elements (the neural network with its neurons and neurotransmitters) grow, as they must quickly and accurately work together to perform such complex work as handling chemicals and electricity, which neurotransmitters deal with.

Thinking: The searching work via a mechanism that uses links or paths of associations with words is, for the most part, the basis of thinking. It is an exploring function.

Curiosity may be an attractive force in the search, as if via an antenna it is seeking for a missing part of the path, either its origin or destination. With curiosity, the network becomes abuzz with neurotransmitters seeking to form associations; they look for the docking sites that can link up with past paths. They want to reunite with them through the paths in the memories.

Learning: Such reuniting work with the paths of association by neurotransmitters is largely the basis of learning. It is a tracing function.

Under normal circumstances, the development of learning goes through numerous constraints and disciplines. Constraints exert controls. They are imposed by such forces as culture, establishments, and mentors. I learn by learning the restraints that I am subjected to. I develop the ability to trace my paths conscientiously and to explore new paths with restraints. Disciplines can come from mentors or even from within one's self, like learning the multiplication table. I become proficient in steering the paths for proper tracing. As a result, the network of tracing my paths is shaped accordingly. With an exception of some rare cases of precocious youth, be it a photographic memory or virtuosity in music, I see it is basically in agreement with the known phenomenon that my capacity for learning as well as thinking, or the capacity and the growth of my neural network, is influenced by the development of my character.

Character: My character is really a set of paths that I accumulate from my learning. It can influence which paths to link when searching or exploring by tracing. It grows and changes dynamically through learning or thinking. It can be the source of my drive.

Suppose I have something I really need to accomplish but have not been able to do so because I have been busy. If I realize that the morning hours are the best for my learning because I am physically energetic and mentally clear or alert, I may make an effort to get up and get to it before anything, even before eating. If it is a success, I apply such a discipline to other challenges (or get right to my purpose). If not, I modify the parts that were not helpful. So character is a set of paths that can signal whether my own performance meets my standards or expectations.

Emotions: When I perceive an outcome, it can be far from my original expectation, which is based on my past experiences and logic. The resulting paths can go off illogically onto intuitive levels. By intuitive I mean those paths that I have from my infancy and very nature, namely those with little learned associations. I could imagine neurons getting lost or derailed without rational paths, defaulting to the native settings and native destinations. Thus, strong intuitive paths (such as fight or flight) can block out weak sensing paths that

141

were acquired over time (such as rationality). I conjecture that, as the person's character forms, the extent of such a derailment determines (and is also determined in a feedback by) the type of native feelings and their varying level. If I expect the same level of service from a clerk in a sushi store in Chicago as in Chikugo, Japan, chances are I will be disappointed. But with patience and recall, I eventually come to peace because of the difference in culture. If I think my neighbor will be a responsible citizen but he behaves otherwise, I may get miffed rather easily or, depending on his behavior, even act hostile toward him. So in terms of the current perspectives, my emotions touch consciousness in primeval manners without words, while my thoughts employ words; either way, the paths bring out the associated feelings accordingly.

Intelligence: After the neural network starts growing, there accumulates a facility to execute the actions of learning or thinking (tracing or searching) with some guiding paths containing memories of controls and criteria. Neurotransmitter signals travel certain paths and reach their designated destinations according to such guidance. The accumulating capacity is intelligence.

If I aspire to be a successful entrepreneur in commercial real estate, I have the capacity or intelligence to strive for it by learning the skill and knowledge. I would feel I have the right to be able to learn it, as I know that is what I want. In learning it, I have a choice as to how I can achieve it. That is to say, I realize thinking is a choice. There are many ways to think. So what I learn over time based on such thinking choices provides me with a set of guiding paths. Intelligence, therefore, is a self-generating learning and thinking function.

How do I characterize myself if I do not use intelligence when I need to? I might label it as a stupid action.

Stupidity: But how do I define that in the present context? I define that to be the failure to search for paths that would inform me of the *consequences* of a line of thought or action. It can happen to anyone, anytime, and therefore it does not describe a person's overall quality.

Music: Music has the power to calm or "reset" the path search confusion in the brain. (See *Musicophilia* by Oliver Sacks, for example.) Confused links get totally refreshed (or "rewired") by linked sounds of melodies. How the linking is done, especially if it is appealing to our emotion, is an exercise in creative thinking. To the normal mind, the creative paths can be very soothing, which means our body can achieve a chemical equilibrium. Depending on the type of music, it is not hard to associate the tone of the music with the mood swing. The implication, then, is that just as annoying noise can irritate us, great music can be therapeutic. The masterful pieces by Chopin, for example, are awesome in terms of paths that very few people could match. The awe can restore a sense of clarity in humble inquisitiveness: *how* could he ever come up with that melody? So when I seek a creative path, I imagine a ride with classical music notes. When I hear an unexpectedly creative piece, I try to mimic it in my search, which resembles a scene of a serene space voyage from the movie *2001: A Space Odyssey*. It is surprisingly helpful and effective in selecting creative paths.

It is easy to see why stores play music to get their customers into a mood for shopping; that is on the emotional level. How about on the thinking level? When I am in a mood to do some heavy-duty analysis in mathematics, I tend to prefer listening to a piece by Bach or Handel because the overall abstractness somehow sets my mind "clearer." If I want to feel creative, I prefer Mozart or Vivaldi because of its whimsical nature. If I want to feel relaxed, I seek a piece from the Beatles band (naturally!). Now then, if I want to switch my mood from one of the above three to another, I could play appropriate music to help choose directions for a desired path.

Elucidation: Among the thinking functions, elucidation perhaps stands out as a crown jewel. (It may be clear by now that I enjoy using this word a lot!) A demand for elucidation ups the ante in neural challenges by calling for a neural network search for specifically illuminating words and ideas. Querying helps sharply define the path through the neurons that will produce the precise articulation that elucidation requires. Discovering how to learn or how to think requires maturity in linking words with precision in the brain.

For example, suppose I have been asked to select a candidate for a job position. I need to elucidate the job's requirements and the candidates' qualifications. Why? Because then I can make a better decision about hiring the best candidate for the job. Neural paths for my thinking are made clearer thanks to the elucidation.

Maturity: This is an important part of character that greatly influences how learning or thinking is performed through path selections.

Humility, for example, can open more doors to learning as neurons look for learning paths with less influence from past guidance. The idea of self-reliance highlighted by such philosophers as Ralph Waldo Emerson and Henry David Thoreau is another example of maturity. It encourages a criterion of self-search in ideas and reasons with discipline and independence. Paths are selected with an emphasis for such attitudes. Listening ability is another example of personal growth. Peter Drucker, known for his management ideas, was supposedly such a great listener that he often saw answers in what his client was saying. What that means is that paths are obtained by hearing what the client wishes, or by summing up the client's goal.

Goal: In pursuit of any accomplishment, the goal should be the most critical element, as it defines your ultimate destination. The neurotransmitters are energized by having such a purpose. The goal should be a search for purpose or meaning, not for rewards.

As Viktor Frankl noted in his fight for survival during his ordeal at a Nazi concentration camp, a drive for materialistic rewards for survival is fragile even for an additional day of life. The determined search for meaning was enduring, guiding him as a lighthouse during his struggle to survive.[50] Similar to his search for meaning, the key to learning or thinking is its goal that is associated with that learning or thinking, the very reason you go through the trouble of learning or thinking. A goal forms a strong chain for the paths. Without a goal, the signals in the neural network are meandering. With goals, they are determined to line up in forceful motivation for the purpose of reaching the goal.

Desperate and destitute, Manuel and John Inadomi set their goals to provide for each of their families. The force behind their motivation was so strong that a loss of their wealth due to World War II internment never destroyed their will to continue their efforts. Having a goal is the lifeline for learning and thinking as well. The practical significance shows up in the fact that a how-to search is dependent on the choice of goal.

Evolutionary Nature: What is evident is that all this work for the growth of the organic entity, the neural network, takes time. It registers new words and paths from experiences. They are added to the

---

50 Viktor E. Frankl, *Man's Search for Meaning* (Touchstone Books, 1984).

network's infrastructure. Character is formed and reformed. Trials and tribulations, and successes and failures, which result from acting on thoughts accumulate as part of the intelligence. Memories or past sets of paths fade away, and new associations are created. New goals are set, and the growth cycle continues throughout the length of life. It is part of the organic life's nature. If I look back at my own growth, I can begin to appreciate the lengthy evolutionary fact. It provides me with a chance to reflect on my own progress, which is basically a tracing (or learning) action. And I can reflect in this manner because I learned how to learn. My neural network has evidently built a decent structure of traceable paths!

Mind and Matter: Finally a hard topic about our mind. As is well-known, Western thinking tends to treat mind and matter separately.[51] Some Eastern philosophy, like that of Buddha, though lacking the precision of the West, considers the mind differently, as part of holistic nature ("The mind is everything. What you think you become."[52]). My perspectives, however, might explain that yet differently, that is, in a combined manner.

First we get impulses and register them in our memory as ideas and thoughts. Linked paths enable neural signals to pass through our neural network to activate the associated memories to create and recreate thoughts. Some are associated with words; others are less so, more like feelings. Feelings are triggered first by innate or primal reactionary signal transmissions, such as fear, hunger, and anger. Music is an example of expressing that feeling in sound; literature is done with words, and arts with more general objects of all kinds.

---

51 Jacques Barzun, *From Dawn to Decadence* (New York: Harper Perennial, 2000), 200.
52 *BrainyQuotes*, s.v. "Buddha," BookRags Media Network, www.brainyquote.com/quotes/authors/b/buddha.html

When we search for paths to cognize such a resulting activity, what we have is our consciousness. Our soul is the organic consciousness faculty. Thus, the mind is an organic function, a set of organs that enable signals to travel through the neural network. A feeling is a result of signals traversing linked paths to create a reaction in memory in the organic substance called the brain. The mind then integrates the results of the reaction in memory in terms of neural signals, that is, in essence, organic substance in the neural network.

Things are perhaps getting a bit too philosophical to continue the theme of fun. Nonetheless, these are explanations of what is already well-known, expressed in terms of the ideas behind the perspectives. In a way I am trying to make the point that when learning or thinking, what takes place in the brain can be, and also should be, viewed as organic activities of the neural network. A ramification of that point is that because we are all born, for the most part, equal organic entities, little credence should be given to the notion that one person is "smarter" than another. With work and care, the neural network should grow to whatever extent desired for anyone who really wants to learn and develop.

If I am to expand the explanations to those problems that challenge us, there might be something of undiscovered value. Below are a few cases.

Thought Exploration

These are the principal thoughts underlying my perspectives. Understanding them as such naturally spurs further thoughts and ideas. In my case I have entertained the following future thoughts. I selected a few in the hope that my points might inspire a fresh look from different reference angles and open different windows to explore.

Malfunctions in the Process

There are some symptoms I can view as malfunctions in learning or thinking in terms of the neural network. I view them as malfunctions because I can fix them (usually). To fix them I first need to describe what they are and how they impact my learning or thinking.

Emotional interruption—search for paths in the network is halted
- Anger—due to overrunning normal paths by unexpected "mistreatment" by others
- Depression—due to overload with associated "dark" paths, such as sadness, helplessness, and disappointment

Can I learn to block these so I can resume my learning or thinking? Yes, I have been able to, and more and more effectively as I age! I follow the five steps, and for the most part, I can overcome such impediments to thinking or learning.

Physiological overload—the network is paralyzed
- Headaches—overload on path search with energy of oppression, threats and worries; warning messages sent out may be causing the pain.
- Panic attacks—allergy-like symptoms with similar energy attacking the weakest point of the physiology; warning messages sent out may be overreacting potentially triggering a wrong fight, like histamine causing allergy reactions.

I view pains as physiological warnings. They warn that the *way* I am thinking is causing some pain in the neural network. As with histamine, the neural system reacts to elements such as fear in a protective or immunizing mode. I can try to retreat as far as necessary to find a better way. It usually takes some coordinated effort, both mental and physiological, as the pain can last some time. It takes time for the body to "heal" or regain the original state. The best time to combat physiological overload is when a sign of malfunction is first detected. Find in advance a toolbox full of techniques to deal with the problem, such as moving to a different atmosphere and switching your thinking. For example, you might tackle more pleasant or really interesting thinking activities or indulge in less taxing mental pastimes, such as entertainment, music, or simpler therapeutic exercises. When I recall my own cases, I note a good pattern: the release of pain is correlated to my effort to imagine and emulate a joyous state of mind as if I were able to control the source or let go of my involvement, my "responsible" part. The pain reliever appears to be *how* I think about the situation.

Mental misdirection—search for paths is misdirected
- Lying—choosing paths of deliberate fiction
- Bigotry—shutting down openings for paths
- Deceit—choosing paths of falseness
- Narcissism—choosing paths of self-interest, self-reward

It is not hard to see, hopefully, that these have a lot to do with the confirmation and review steps. I ask myself a lot of questions related to the steps, such as whether I will later regret not having done my very best. As long as I am eager to learn by reviewing my own performance, and confirm my goal and my desire to reach that goal sincerely, then I know I have a high chance of success in battling these misdirected path selections.

As I said earlier, these are things I can usually fix as they are usually and mostly within my control.

Cultural or traditional forces around us are usually harder to control. For instance, in those ubiquitous electronic gizmos around us we find great pleasure. These devices usually demand hand and eye coordination, quickness in pattern recognition, and little search effort with the use of words, especially those of *why*, *how*, and *what*. If the neural network is predisposed to those activities, it is natural that searching activities become less attuned to deliver when needed, meaning more pain accompanies learning and thinking. If I feel compelled by cultural forces to use those devices to keep up with my family members and their kids, how can I expect my neurotransmitters to get enough exercise!? Entertainment is the mere receipt of stimuli and does not involve work on neural path searches, and it is therefore degenerative to the network's overall health.

There are some remedial actions I suggest, however, in the following two cases. Both cases show a potential danger to thorough thinking.

Adventure 1: Words as Well as Numbers

I recognize that a majority of the celebrated human accomplishments throughout history, especially those of late, are based on the use of numbers. Science and math use numbers, and with them high-profile breakthroughs are created with huge, awe-inspiring implications.

Now, when I consider that, I often sense a built-in bias of sorts for numbers; the use of numbers is easier than that of words. One result of that bias is that the areas far from the reach of benefit of numbers, such as philosophy, law, and literary communication, do not seem to receive their share of opportunity for advancement. I believe it is important to encourage diction, rhetoric, and literary skills in much the same way that the numeric skills are encouraged. Better character is developed with the use of more words than numbers.

Develop a rational mind with words supported by numbers, not the other way around. We need to put Confucius and Rene Descartes together in one place so they can hash out an addendum to *Discourse on Method* that is applicable to nonquantitative disciplines! We need Gauss with the word power of Shakespeare so Gauss can start working with elucidation in words, just as he did with numbers.

Recently I saw a trend to employ metrics or indices to monitor such things as corporate performance and social work. It was a trend like a fad, in some cases, and the metrics were used to evaluate more than what they were designed for. One has a nicely coined term, "Six Sigma." Another catchword is *dashboard*, to present metrics in a dazzling format. In some cases there is so much of it that it's easy to be flooded and forget what the main business goal is; a fancy presentation becomes the main business task. As is commonly recognized, though, those things are designed to assist the business. One of the well-known father figures of this idea is W. Edwards Deming. Many books have been written to popularize his idea. Motorola, Inc. actually succeeded in producing the highest quality products using its own well-known guideline called the Six Sigma method, alluded to above.

At any rate, in an interview with the *Wall Street Journal* some time ago, W. Edwards Deming was asked if we should work toward a goal to reduce workplace injuries by 50 percent per year over the next ten years. His answer was,

> "No, no, no. The goal should be reduced workplace injuries. Put a figure on it, then you're wrong. That would be destructive. You only get what the system will deliver. The goal doesn't help you deliver."[53]

Now exactly what did he mean by that? Yes, it's time to think.

First, he believed in measuring, all right. He was a statistician to begin with. What he objected to, however, was drawing wrong conclusions from those measurements. The goal of the task here was to reduce workplace injuries, which was far more than just achieving some quota. Just because a quota was achieved did not mean the goal was achieved.

Because we tend to put things in numbers (for such reasons as convenience and presentation impact via simplification), we tend to feel we accomplish our goal when we achieve the numbers. But Deming knew that numbers would not do the whole job. He had already understood the limitation of statistics in view of goal setting. That is to say, numbers really cannot fully express the overall goal. It takes deep thinking to express our goal, which will require descriptions with both words and numbers. A use of a metric would only be a piece of a bigger entirety. Deming was aware that setting an easy-to-explain numerical target would not suffice.

Yes, it is good to use measurable quantities to help achieve a goal. A prevailing thought is that if we cannot measure, we haven't got it

---

53 "Deming's Demons," Workplace in Managing Change Section, *The Wall Street Journal*, June 4, 1990.

yet. That's fine, but I do not necessarily agree, because a measurement is a snapshot of the situation viewed from one specific angle. It takes a lot of thinking to size the whole picture more accurately. There are different goals. So that means there is a need to consider different levels of goals, from the "lowest" to the "highest." By the highest goal, I mean the one that brings us to the real objective. By such logic, then, it should include the lower goals. If the goal is to reduce workplace injuries, then achieving that necessarily implies achieving a lower number of injuries. The reverse does not necessarily imply achieving our real or highest goal. (To some, this discussion probably sounds more like a text from a course in logic!)

I respect the field of statistics as I championed its use at Cummins by encouraging the engineers to use statistical views.[54] I know what numbers can and cannot express; perhaps this sensitivity is tied to my own cultural background—the shunning of the black and white mentality. Words are better tools for me if I am not really trying to measure anything.

Where am I going with this? I am asserting numbers are important, but words are just as important as numbers! I feel the time is overdue to balance the potentials of elucidation through accurate diction with numbers. The reason is that numbers are *but one* representation of a part of the bigger spectrum of paths. Numbers cannot replace such a spectrum. Only well-thought-out words can illuminate truly guiding paths to the ultimate goal. Moreover, the use of such words helps deliver logic or intelligence, which is an essential part of the humanity. For an eloquent commentary along this line, see Jacques Barzun's *Begin Here*[55].

---

54 Mitsuo Ogata, *Engineers' Manual of Probability and Statistical Methods* (Columbus, IN: Cummins Engine Company, 1975).
55 Jacques Barzun, *Begin Here* (Chicago, IL: University of Chicago Press, 1992).

The second example is a bit more sinister in that human activities, especially as a collective unit, can tend to be abusive. *Group* thinking or learning is evidently far harder than in the individual case because it is that much harder to control.

Adventure 2: More Checks and Balances

The concept of "checks and balances," part of the foundation of today's government, is well established. Because of its enduring reliability in protecting the "good" from the "bad," I believe it can be applied to our effort in attaining the genuine purposes.

There are plenty of issues in public affairs. From financial deficits to corruption, from health care to education, from gas drilling to immigration, they present a constant challenge for learning or thinking. In recent election years, I have seen evidence of special groups of people with financial resources and interests influencing the thinking of the leaders right where I live. The elected leaders seem to be swayed rather easily according to the prevailing wind. The result is an abuse of authority.

Unlike dealing with one person's goal, dealing with goals for a group of people can be a huge challenge. There again, however, citing the highest goal to recall the purpose and meaning should be the key to successful learning and thinking for the group of people. The confirm and discover steps applied to a group can benefit from the review step for an individual in that the character of the group can employ such a concept of checks and balances. I could observe, ask, confirm, discover, and review so that I could voice the best decision on these issues to my public representative. It is a tall order indeed because I need to keep up my drive or energy for the sake of the people as a whole. Will the elected officials and their leader be able to serve the people in a similar manner? At least, they are supposed to serve the majority.

When dealing with a group of legislatures having conflicting interests among them, a solution might be to install a strong reminder of checks and balances in the five-step approach. They need to see for themselves that they are monitoring the integrity in the process of legislating public laws. Indeed, such a reminder should be built-in to ensure automatic kicking-in of a safeguard mechanism. For example, if legislation like the Affordable Care Act is to succeed, there needs to be an assurance that an abusive entitlement mentality will not destroy the well-intended goal of helping the needy. There needs to be a safety valve to curtail cost overruns because uncertainties or risks are always there. Politicians cannot foresee future events. They need to think well for their constituents with respect to their genuine goal by incorporating safety mechanisms into the "system"; thus, a motto for them to remember might be "In Checks and Balances We Trust."

So I believe there is a benefit in revisiting these issues that challenge us to learn or think more successfully from the frame of reference represented by my approach. And as I mentioned before, I feel enthusiastic about the apparently endless potential of my perspectives. I can keep on growing. At least in theory, that implies I could say:

I Could Become a Genius

In a very specialized area or field, I could grow to be able to search for paths that no one has ever thought of because I discovered how to search for paths. Of course, in some rare cases, I can stop thinking or forget how to think entirely due to some unfortunate situations, such as an injured mind or mental illness. In normal cases I definitely think it is a frontier I can explore without end.

Imagine sitting next to Gauss or Einstein and listening to his questions when he was young, specifically to his words, diction, elucidation, paths, criteria, etc. It would have been an eye-opening experience since the paths and the searches he was discovering were completely new and original! Likewise, imagine sitting next to Thomas Jefferson when he was composing the draft of the Declaration of Independence. How did he think about those amazingly powerful ideas, and how did he come up with how to say what he wanted to say!?

I am in awe when I try to fathom the goal, the ambition, the will, and the desire to attain what those men in history wanted. It impresses me so much when I think about their power to elucidate, look for paths of ideas, and stay focused on their ultimate goals with energy, discipline, and passion. They were geniuses all right.

They were. I am not.

And yet what essential differences are there between them and me organically? To be sure, that is unknown. Perhaps their neural networks were the equivalent of an autobahn early on, even from birth. My network was built into a mere state road over a long time. But now that I know *how* (at least somewhat) to duplicate their thought *processes*, I feel, with determination, I should be able to become a creative pioneer in my field of choice in time!

There is one more observation I would like to make regarding the way learning or thinking happens in the brain. As I mentioned, words are linked, and paths are searched for words with certain criteria and control. When a search is completed, the network recognizes the paths. All that sounds like a complex process in view of our "limited" cerebral memory capacity. What if we created a similar mechanism on the computer? That is, can I entertain the following?

Use of the Computer in Learning and Thinking

I realize this is a rather daunting and commonly challenged phraseology. The computer will not help us learn or think! Perhaps or perhaps not. At least I can venture and explore possibilities. Here is my outline for an idea that might have some merit in view of the preceding observation.

First I see how words, content, paths, and guidelines help me think. So I start with words and define them by a set of other words associated with them. It can emulate a child's learning of words, or the way Helen Keller learned words.[56] The collection of words becomes like a dictionary or, with some order, even the words in *Roget's Thesaurus*. There could be a million-plus words in the English language.

To link words, as with numbers and mathematical operations performed on the numbers, I could set up schemes regarding how the words are associated by way of such rules as grammar and definitions. As a tool to link those words, I could use a similar method as the linking tool known as the universal record locator used in the web or HTML (HyperText Markup Language). There could be some other method, of course. Abbreviated as URL, a uniform resource locator is a basic mechanism for linking content on the Internet.

---

56 Carolyn Lyon Remington, *Vibrant Silence* (Rochester, NY: The Lawyers Cooperative Publishing Company, 1965).

The URLs and *tags*, or their local version, could be used as a basis for paths. Rules could be built to emulate neurotransmitter docking phenomena.

Searching and tracing of paths, those of thinking and learning, may be extensions of the search engines we already use on the Internet. Rules used for searching, such as frequent visits to sites, may be expanded to incorporate other criteria, such as ethical values and moral standards.

At least that is the start of a design to implement my conjecture. The idea is so that I could reach out to discover unknown or inconceivable paths beyond what the ordinary mind could in much shorter time. Isn't it fun to imagine such a possibility?!

It may take some time to create even a prototype, but I believe it can be done. I elaborate it a bit further in the Appendix with some technical treatment.

Conclusion

When I picture Albert Einstein performing his thought experiments to ponder strange ideas or search for unknown paths, he probably used his imagination to expand his neural network capacity. His ability to imagine was phenomenal, fast, and unusual. It would be amazing to see all those neural signals fly around to find new paths to form new ideas.

Though impressive and exotic his cerebral function might have appeared to most of us ordinary humans, the perspectives discussed in this book might challenge such a verdict. At least I believe the five-step approach is helpful in that regard.

In reaching the end of this book, I would like to close it with the following comment.

I began this book by saying we should all be able to enjoy learning and thinking. If we are not, we are not doing it right. That led me to investigate what would be the key to doing it right.

The key was to discover the process of how to learn. Or, in terms of the terminology used in this book, the key was to search for the process of tracing paths to link up with the words and ideas that have already been understood. When a process was found, it became easy and fun; the process guided the steps for understanding or stated more generally, learning.

I went on to say that the next challenge was to be able to replicate the task of finding such a process at all times. It was usually a challenge because of various pressures and constraints such as time and commitments, or simply because of the pure difficulty of dealing with unknown territory. Moreover, it was a slow learning process. Yes, it was the same *learning* challenge all over again!

As expected, there was a process for that, too. The discussion eventually revealed that the process involved deeper interactions for how we grow as mature and intelligent human beings. It was really no mystery, but there was a complex interplay of how we get our learning and thinking done. A lot of it boiled down to "common sense." As long as we communicate in words of our language of choice, I saw such an ability to communicate as one of the essential ways of learning or thinking, and we need to keep capacity at full power. And how we used it in our thoughts—actively or inactively, sincerely or maliciously—was partly determined by our own personal character, so that improving our character became another key element. That encompassed many things, such as our ambitions and search for meaning. The further the target we aim for, the greater the accomplishment we evidently could realize. But the most fundamental requirement was our physiological well-being, which nurtures our ability to learn and think. In the end it was up to each of us to work to orchestrate those key elements toward our improvement and growth.

Such perspectives led me to outline a process for nurturing proficiency in learning how to learn and think in five steps. The essence

further triggered the idea that our language, or more specifically our vocabulary, was the *material medium* for our mind. All along we missed highlighting the connection: mind can be represented by "matter," the alphabetical representation of concepts, or words. Thus the mind is a collection of neural links associated with impressions formed in our cerebral. The key question we face then is how well such a collection can learn to expand through faculties such as curiosity, imagination, and character growth. Our five-step approach presented here is an attempt to provide the how-to for it. We can almost foresee that we can extend our boundaries of mind as long as our physiology lets us. Besides, we have technology to begin an exploration for that!

Of course we need to be smart about how we use our technology, for look around us for a moment. It is not that difficult to see how electronic devices like cell phones can rob us of the opportunity to take the time to think thoroughly and learn well. They demand speed, but thoughts demand search, and that takes time. The dexterity of our fingers receives more training than thinking deeply or widely when communicating in text messages. And the knowledge of vocabulary, due to the constraints of one-finger typing, is probably not in high demand in the technological world. But such a measure as speed is only a partial gauge for the huge potential we have in our physiological and intellectual capacities. We have huge potential in our ability to grow on our own, specifically our ability to learn or think almost limitlessly. Already we are said to perform a far greater number of neural activities than the total number of stars in the entire universe, or the total number of leaves on all the trees in the Amazon.[57] And yet we are known to use, on average, only a third of our brain. If we could use the computer to help remember things, we could hardly imagine what we could do. What

---

57 Bard and Bard, *The Complete Idiot's Guide to Understanding the Brain*, 82.

potential, what a frontier, do we have in our ability to learn and think!

Certainly such growth remains a lifelong effort for each of us. Luckily for us, when we do take a step forward, we get a reward of successful learning or thinking. But for you who endured reading my book to this point, you now know about a key perspective for successful learning or thinking—with one qualifier: as long as your wellness permits! The key perspective is the golden nugget we have been seeking:

1. Be alert to sense what is around you (*Observe*),
2. Be inquisitive to register perceptions genuinely (*Ask*),
3. Be honest to pursue your own purpose (*Confirm*),
4. Inspire and be imaginative in thinking (*Discover*), and
5. Learn to enhance each and all of these abilities (*Review*).

We could almost say that learning is our right including learning how to think. In that effort, we realize knowing the how-to makes it fun. Depending on how genuinely the fun is generated, we can reach the world of imagination and unknowns far and beyond, just as Mozart did in creating his music, just as Einstein did in defying the laws of conventional physics. So in closing, here is my wish to you: may you continue to enjoy pursuing *your cerebral fun.*

Yes, *you* should be able to do just about anything, and *you* could also become a genius!

own performance versus the teacher's. For example, any deviations from the teacher's image can be highlighted for faster learning. The real power of this method comes from mustering all means, visual and audio senses, dynamically and interactively. Today's oscilloscope is minimal in that it can illustrate deviations but is audio only. New options could be developed to visually contrast the native speaker's movements with the student's.

Once we can illustrate how each sound is generated by the collective organs' coordinated work in our body, there should be little difficulty in the initial learning. The student must practice to train his or her skill and coordination until it becomes second nature, that is to say, reflective without much conscious effort.

Appendix Two: Example of High Goal Setting—Encouragement of Learning by Yukichi Fukuzawa

The following excerpts are from *The Autobiography of Yukichi Fukuzawa*.[59] It represents an example of great thinking by setting the highest goal for the thinking. My thesis is that the highest goal is critical because it shapes and guides the thinking activity, influencing the consequential action to execute. The key question is, what should the highest goal be? Usually it takes time or experiences to become capable of distinguishing the level of the goal, whether it still is not the highest feasible. Once the ability is acquired, the discerning naturally becomes easy and fun, opening the door to a motivated state of mind in search of the highest. A good example in the real world is seeking employment: if a job seeker is clear about his or her true intent or the highest goal, that is, the calling, finding a satisfying job becomes easy and even fun.

The autobiography was first published in 1899 by Yukichi Fukuzawa and was later revised and translated by his grandson, Eiichi Kiyooka. His essay "Encouragement of Learning," appears in the Appendix. In order to provide an informative introduction to it and the background, I have elected to include the foreword by the late Carmen Blacker as well. Both are reprinted here with the permission of the publisher.

As you read it, consider the question: if you were Fukuzawa, would you have set your goal to be the *encouragement of learning for the masses*? The fact he chose that as his goal shows his genius.

---

59 Copyright © 1966 Columbia University Press.

FOREWORD

Here is the autobiography of a remarkable man. Fukuzawa Yukichi's life covered the sixty-six years between
1835 and 1901, a period which comprised greater and
more extraordinary changes than any other in the history
of Japan. At the time of his birth Japan was almost
entirely isolated from the outside world, with a hierarchical feudal system based on a Confucian code of morals.
Her notions of warfare were medieval, her economy
largely agricultural, her knowledge of modern science con-
fined to the trickle of Dutch books which found their way
into the country through the trading station at Nagasaki.
At the time of his death Japan was to all effects a modern
state. Her army and navy were so well disciplined and
equipped that six years before they had defeated China
and four years later they were to defeat Russia. She had
a parliament, compulsory education, rapidly growing in-
dustries, and distinguished universities.

For these astonishing changes we can hold responsible
both the impersonal forces of history and the very personal power of certain individual men. Among the latter
Fukuzawa Yukichi was one of the most remarkable. He
is generally acknowledged to have been the leading educa-
tor of the new Japan, the man who above all others explained to his countrymen the ideas behind the dazzling
material evidence of western civilization; who insisted
that it was not enough for Japan merely to have the
"things" of civilization—the trains, the guns, the warships,
the hats, the umbrellas—in order to take her place with

dignity and confidence among the nations of the modern
world. It was also necessary for her to comprehend the
learning which in the West had led to the discovery and
production of these things. And this would require a
drastic reconsideration of some of her most ancient and
unquestioned assumptions about the nature of the universe.

To explain these new and unfamiliar ideas Fukuzawa
wrote voluminously over a period of some thirty years.
He started a newspaper which continued for half a century as one of the great Tokyo dailies. He founded a
school which is one of the largest and most distinguished
universities in Japan.

The autobiography of such a man, a philosopher and a
schoolmaster, might be expected to be perhaps a little dry,
an abstract, inward account of ideas and conflicting principles. Not so this book. From the first page we are
captivated, enthralled by both the author and the tale he
tells.

He starts with his childhood in the small feudal clan of
Nakatsu in Kyushu. We are shown a vanished world,
a small, rigid society governed to an extent almost unim-
aginable today by minute distinctions of hierarchical rank.
Fukuzawa tells us that he always loathed the "narrow
stiffness" of the life there, indeed hated the feudal system
as though it had been his father's murderer. His discontent is not difficult to understand. His family was of
the samurai class, but of a low rank within that class. He
was one of those "lower samurai," in fact, whose im-
poverishment and discontent at this time drove them a
couple of decades later to become the main force behind
the overthrow of the Shogunate. The strict laws of the

no idea that the contents of [my] books would ever be applied to our own social conditions," he wrote. "In short, I was writing my books simply as stories of the West or as curious tales of a dreamland."

It was not until after the upheaval of the Restoration, when the new government had shown itself to be not the collection of ignorant fools which he had feared, but rather a group of able men determined to build up a new Japan on thoroughly modern lines, that Fukuzawa came to realize his true mission in life. This was nothing more nor less than to refashion the whole way of thinking of his country-men. He felt, he wrote towards the end of the book, that he "must take advantage of the moment to bring in more of Western civilization and revolutionise our people's ideas from the roots. Then perhaps it would not be im-possible to form a great nation in this far Orient which would stand counter to Great Britain of the West, and take an active part in the progress of the whole world."

What was it that he found so misguided in the traditional Japanese way of thinking? In an interesting passage he tells us that there seemed to be two important things lack-ing, science and the spirit of independence. The reason why western statesmen governed their countries so suc-cessfully and western businessmen were so successful in commerce and industry, why the people were so patriotic and their family circles so happy, was because their civili-zation was based on the laws of science and the principle of independence. The reason why Japan lay behind in these matters was because her traditional Confucian learn-ing had neglected these two important principles.

For the rest of his life, therefore, Fukuzawa made it his task to promulgate this new philosophy in every way possible—in the teaching in his school, in the policy of his newspaper, in his voluminous writings, in his private life. After the tales of adventure, of foreign travel, of the hidden assassin, which make the early chapters of this book such compelling reading, his life following 1868 settled down to a quieter tenor of writing and teaching. He refused all offers of government employment, for reasons we may read towards the end of the book, and devoted himself in an entirely private capacity to the propagation of his philosophy.

Books and articles appeared from his pen in a steady stream, concerned to point out the shortcomings of the old learning and values, and to propose new principles better suited to the position Japan must play in the modern world. His writings cover an astonishing range. He wrote on ethics, on politics, on economics, on historiography, on international law. He wrote, of course, on the philosophy of science, and the spirit of independent observation and criticism which had led to the rise of such a philosophy in the West. He showed how the old Confucian system of ethics could no longer stand in a society which promoted science, and proposed a new set of values to put in its place. He attacked the old family system, championing particularly the cause of women, and of children oppressed by too demanding canons of filial piety.

Many of his ideas we now take for granted, forgetting the courage that was needed at the time to voice them so clearly. Among his most sensational words were the opening sentences of his book *Gakumon no Susume* (The encouragement of learning): "Heaven never created a man above another nor a man below another." Men might differ in their outward circumstances and conditions,

Nakatsu clan required that in almost every context of daily life the lower samurai should abase themselves before their superiors in feudal rank. The men of Fukuzawa's low status, besides being much poorer, less educated, and more tediously occupied than the upper samurai, were required to prostrate themselves on their faces every time they encountered an upper samurai; to address their superiors with all the resources of the honorific vocabulary while suffering themselves to be addressed in language which was habitually abusive; to speak with a more boorish accent than that used by the samurai of higher rank. The two classes of men were treated in effect like two different species of nature, for marriage between them was strictly forbidden and virtually unknown.

Most of his contemporaries, Fukuzawa tells us in another work of reminiscence, were discontented with their lot, but utterly unable to express their discontent. They would no more dream of trying to rise in the world by entering the ranks of the upper samurai than would a four-legged beast hope to fly like a bird. They accepted all the distinctions of feudal rank as though these were part of the fixed and immutable order of nature rather than the invention of man.

Fukuzawa was one of the very few who cared nothing for feudal propriety, thinking it no disgrace to go shopping in broad daylight. "Why should I not?" he asked himself. Nor had he any reverence for the things generally accounted holy. Secretly, in order to test their efficacy, he trampled on the sacred paper charms and put them to vile uses in the lavatory. The fact that nothing terrible ensued from these outrages made him a lifelong skeptic.

To escape from the tedium and petty formality of the

clan was his one thought. His chance eventually came, when he was nineteen years old, in the form of the western studies which were later to become his life's work. But in 1854 it was not from any lofty ambitions for the future that he set out for Nagasaki to learn gunnery, but simply because it was a convenient excuse for getting away. "I would have been glad to study a foreign language or the military art or anything else if only it gave me a chance to go away . . . I still remember how I swore to myself that like a bullet shot out of the gun's muzzle I would never come back." He spat on the ground as he walked away.

His pursuit of western studies eventually took him to Osaka, where he entered the school of the celebrated scholar Ogata. His account of his Dutch studies in Osaka is one of the most fascinating chapters in the book. The Ogata students were poor and unconventional. Most of them had pawned their swords. Indoors they usually went naked except at meals and at classes. In the streets they were so rowdy that the citizens were careful to give them a wide berth. Yet at their Dutch studies they worked with a fierce enthusiasm which made no distinction between night and day. "I would be reading all day," Fukuzawa tells us here, "and when night came I did not think of going to bed. . . . We could not have studied harder." The difficulties they encountered can scarcely be realized by us today. Among eighty or ninety students there was only one Dutch dictionary. The college library consisted of ten Dutch books of science, which the student, once he had mastered the rudiments of grammar, had to wait his turn to copy laboriously with a brush or quill.

What was the motive which prompted Fukuzawa and

Appendices

The intent of the five Appendices, besides as reference to the preceding body of the book, is to provide examples or tools for fun learning and thinking.

Appendix One: Learning a Spoken Language Using an Interactive Graphic Interface

Part of the hardship in learning a foreign language lies in the lack of the how-to: how to learn it, especially how to pronounce the foreign words. Teaching methods usually rely on the student's ability to listen and repeat the words on his or her own. Yes, practice is necessary. However, my thesis is that the rote method can become fun and easy once the methodology is amplified by other aids, such as visual information. To encourage such an approach, it is helpful to think differently by shifting the perspective that learning a spoken language is a dynamic and interactive learning process involving the facial and mouth anatomy.

As I mentioned earlier, spoken languages naturally use sound, with certain facial and other movements, such as the lips, tongue, and jaws. The verbal skill of speaking a second language then requires the ability to reproduce the sound in the same manner as the native speakers.[58] Besides the sound, that includes the facial and anatomical movements. Many computer-aided tools exist today to assist the sound portion. However, there is none yet that can display the movements to the student in an interactive manner as in 3-D. It is important to provide such an aid as part of the learning.

Looking only at the audio side of the challenge, we can treat it as a task of audio production, much like that of learning music. However, what is not explicitly revealed in that approach is the hidden movements of the mouth parts that any native speaker is capable of. The sounds are often triggered by complex interworking of the internal mouth movements. Nonnative speakers do not learn that easily.

Thus, the student of the foreign tongue needs to learn how the natives speak from such a viewpoint, with great attention to the inner movements of the mouth. Sound reproduced in such a way, with little emulation, is not entirely true to the native sound. Accents are one example of that. An experimental teaching of this vocal type was performed by Silas Mosley. I was one of his students, and I benefited a great deal from learning how the sound was produced.

With today's technology we could create a computer application capable of displaying the intricate interplay of the moving parts in the mouth and on the face via a 3-D graphical function. If interactive display is not easily attainable, then at least we could show how the teacher's movements interact in 3-D animation.

The key test is the resultant sound reproduced at the end. The student should be able to improve the results by studying his or her

---

58 Partial information about this can be seen in such books as *Merriam-Webster's Guide to Pronunciation*.

but in the matter of their "rights," their claim to life, property, and human dignity, all were equal. We now take these principles for granted as fundamental to the democratic way of life. But in Japan in 1872 they caused a great outcry. They contradicted entirely the traditional political philosophy which assumed that human society was a natural hierarchy in which all men were by nature unequal.

His stress on science and the spirit of independence we now regard as essential to our conception of valid knowledge. But in the early 1870s in Japan it was something unfamiliar and strange, requiring an entirely new attitude to the things of the external world. How rare indeed was the spirit of independence when Fukuzawa was young we can judge from the first chapter of this book. He seems to have been the only member of his community who questioned the rigid conventions of the hierarchy. The moral code based on the principles of "independence and self-respect" which he formulated at the turn of the century strikes us now as sound and decent common sense. Yet when it first appeared in 1900 it was attacked as the subversive doctrine which had led to the horrors of the French Revolution.

As compassionate and sensible also seem Fukuzawa's pleas for a new spirit in the family, in which the members should live together like a "group of friends," bound by ties not of hierarchical duty but of mutual love and affection. His call for respect for the rights of women, for a more reasonable treatment of their position in society than that accorded them for so long by the odious *Onna Daigaku,* is now accepted without cavil in all civilized countries.

We are too often apt to accept our common stock of wisdom, forgetting the vision and courage which were needed for its discovery. Fukuzawa's contribution to the wisdom of Japan does not strike us now as recondite. It is built into the whole structure of our lives. But, as the Chinese reformer Liang Ch'i Ch'ao said of him, together with Voltaire and Tolstoy, "If these men had not lived, it is doubtful whether their countries could have advanced." Had Fukuzawa not lived, the heritage of Japan would be the poorer. For, however we may choose to define greatness, we must surely include the qualities of vision beyond one's time and of the moral courage to voice what one has seen. Fukuzawa possessed both these qualities, and the extra one of lucidity. He conveyed his unfamilar ideas not in the erudite language so fashionable among scholars but in words that any housemaid could understand.

We are happy to find from this book that he was also very human. Possibly because the book was dictated to a secretary rather than carefully planned and composed, we feel as we read that we are listening to a friend talking. Relaxed and spontaneous, he reminisces of the adventures of his youth among scenes long vanished, recalls odd conversations with his friends, tells confidentially of his hopes and fears. Vignettes from the past well up in his memory, and stay for long afterwards in our own. We recall the scene in the Shōgun's castle on the eve of the Restoration, with the Shōgun's retainers, their usual strict etiquette forgotten, sprawling in the exquisite rooms talking politics as though they were mad or drunk. Or the scenes in Ogata's school, with the students, naked and dirty, poring with fierce concentration over Dutch treatises on anatomy and chemistry. Or the ferocious warrior who came to Fukuzawa's school straight from the last battle of the Restoration, girt with swords and strange trophies. Or the dissipated student whom Fukuzawa ordered to sit up all night in self-reflection, and whom he afterwards regretted having roughly shaken in anger. Or the old beggar woman whose lice and fleas Fukuzawa's mother used compassionately to catch and kill. And throughout, the figure of the author, becoming stronger as we read, more genuinely human, more three-dimensionally companionable and knowable as he speaks.

Professor Eiichi Kiyooka could have made this memorable translation from a sheer delight in the book itself. But for him there is an extra tie. He is Fukuzawa's grandson and has that special insight which comes from a true "sympathy" in the most literal sense of "feeling with" the writer of the book. Fukuzawa would certainly have been glad, as he looked back over his early struggles to learn English, to see that his efforts had borne fruit in such a felicitous command of the English language in his own grandson. Still more glad that these talents should have been used to bring *Fukuō Jiden* (The Autobiography of the Aged Fukuzawa) to the English-speaking world.

CARMEN BLACKER

Cambridge, England
July, 1965

ENCOURAGEMENT OF LEARNING

The First Essay, 1872

BY FUKUZAWA YUKICHI

INTRODUCTORY NOTE. This essay was Fukuzawa's first attempt a
expressing his own ideas and its influence on the thinking of the Jap
nese people was unprecedented. Because newspapers and maga-
nes had not yet gained wide circulation, this essay was brough
it in pamphlet form, and the public took to it "like the thirsty to
ater." Some 200,000 copies were sold. Happy with the success
the first essay, Fukuzawa went on to publish a series of seven
en essays, all called "Encouragement of Learning," between 1872
d 1876.

Previous to this essay, Fukuzawa had written some widely read
oks, such as *Seiyō Jijō* (Things Western), and he had already
en recognized as a man well informed on Western civilization
it with the publication of '"Encouragement of Learning," Fuku-
wa established himself as a thinker and an intellectual leader of
w Japan. There followed a torrent of publications from his
n which led the nation in its great evolution to modernity.

It is interesting to note that this first essay contains practically
erything that Fukuzawa was to discuss in his subsequent works,
ch as the meaning of education and learning, the dignity of an
lividual, freedom and independence, etc. And, very significantly,
: very first line of the first essay, "Heaven never created a man
ove another . . . ," is the most quoted of Fukuzawa's sayings.
The language used in this essay is very quaint. For instance,
: word Heaven as used here has no religious meaning at all.
day the word Nature would be used, but in 1872 the Japanese
rd for Nature had not come into general use. Also, Fukuzawa

was not writing for the intellectuals alone but for the general populace of Japan as well. Fukuzawa once said that he always tried to write so clearly that an uneducated woman from the countryside would understand the words when they were read to her from the next room through the paper door. And so he chose to use everyday expressions of that time in order to reach the general people who knew nothing other than feudalism.

In spite of the quaintness and the outmoded expressions, the basic ideas in this essay are as fresh and virile to men of today as they were to those of 1872. There were many other scholars who advocated new thoughts, but Fukuzawa was foremost in force and clarity of expression and above all in reaching a wide circle of people. It is certain that there has never been in all the history of Japan an essay which compares with this one in its influence on the Japanese people.

February 20, 1960   EIICHI KIYOOKA

Encouragement of Learning

"Heaven never created a man above another nor a man below another," it is said. Therefore, when men are born, Heaven's idea is that all men should be equal to all other men without distinction of high and low or noble and mean, but that they should all work with body and mind, with dignity worthy of the lords of creation, which they are, in order to take all things in the world for the fulfillment of their needs in clothing, food, and dwelling, freely but without obstructing others, so that each can live happily through life.

However, taking a wide view of this human world, we find wise men and ignorant men, rich men and poor men, men of importance and men of little consequence, their differences like those of the cloud and the slime. Why should all this be? The reason is apparent. In the *Jitsugokyō* it is said, "If a man does not study, he will have no knowledge. A man without knowledge is a fool." The distinction between the wise and the foolish comes from whether they have studied or not.

In society there are difficult tasks and easy tasks. Those who undertake difficult tasks are called men of high standing and those who undertake easy tasks are called men of low standing. All the tasks in which one must use his mind and which involve much worry are difficult, and those in which one labors with hands and legs are easy. And so, physicians, scholars, government officials, or big merchants and big farmers who employ many serving men are to be called men of high standing and importance.

When a man is high in standing and importance, his house will naturally be wealthy and, from the viewpoint of lowly people, he will appear to be high beyond their reach. But looking into the root of it all, we will find that the difference comes merely from whether the man has learning or not, and that there are no Heaven-made distinctions. The proverb says, "Heaven does not give riches to men, but gives it to the labor of men." Therefore, as I have said before, a man is not born with rank or riches. Only those who strive for learning and are capable of reasoning will become men of rank and riches while those without learning will become poor and lowly.

Learning does not mean knowing strange words or reading old, difficult literature or enjoying poems and writing verses and such accomplishments, which are of no real use in the world. These accomplishments give much pleasure to the human mind and they have their own values, but they are not to be valued and worshiped as much as the usual run of scholars has tried to make out. Since time immemorial, there have been very few scholars in Chinese classics who were good household providers or merchants who were accomplished in poetry and yet clever in business. For this reason merchants and farmers become concerned when their sons take to learning seriously, thinking that their fortunes will eventually be ruined. This is natural in anxious parents, and proves that this kind of learning is far removed from and quite useless to daily life.

Therefore, this kind of learning without real use should be left to other days and one's best efforts should be given to real learning that is near to men's everyday use—for instance, the forty-seven letters of the alphabet, the composition of letters, bookkeeping, the abacus, and the use of scales. Advancing farther, there will be many subjects to be taken up: Geography is a sort of story of and guide to Japan and all the countries of the world; Natural Philosophy is the study of the nature and the function of all things under the heavens; History is a detailed chronology and studies the conditions of every country in the world, past and present; Economics explains the management of a household and of a country and of the world; Ethics gives the natural principles for a man's conduct of himself and with his fellow men and shows how he should behave in society.

For the study of these subjects, one should read the translations of Western books. In writing one may let the Japanese alphabet suffice in most cases. If there should be a youth with a promise in scholarship, let him learn the "letters written sideways" and let him grasp the fundamentals in even one field or one subject, and according to these let him investigate the principles of things near him, and thus let him fulfil the need of every day. Such is Jitsugaku (Scientific Knowledge or Real Learning) for all men, which should be generally imbibed without distinction of high or low in society. Only after this, should men pursue the separate ways of samurai, farmer, artisan, and merchant, and the household business of each. In this way a man may attain his independence, a house its independence, and the nation too will attain independence.

In the pursuit of learning, the important thing is to know one's proper limitations. The nature of a man as he is born is not bound or restricted; a man as an adult man and a woman as an adult woman should be free and unrestrained in their actions. However, by stressing freedom alone without regard to one's proper limitations, one is most liable to fall into waywardness and licentiousness. What is meant by limitations is to conform to the reason of Heaven and humanity and to attain one's own freedom without infringing upon that of other men.

The boundary line between freedom and waywardness lies in whether one infringes on others or not. For instance, when one is using one's own money, it may seem that one is free to indulge in wine and women and to abandon oneself to licentiousness. But it is not so by any means. One man's licentiousness will become the temptation of many men, causing the general degeneration of the society and the disruption of education. Even if the money he spends is his, his sin cannot be pardoned.

The problems of freedom and independence exist with a nation as much as they do with an individual man. Since ancient times, Japan has been an island country far to the east of the Asian continent, not associating with foreign countries, living on its own produce, and never being sensible of want. But since the Americans came in the Kaei Era, foreign trade and intercourse began and developed to the state we see today. There have been arguments of many kinds even after the opening of the ports, some advocating loudly the closing of the ports and the expulsion of foreigners. However, these arguments take a very narrow point of view like that of the proverbial frog at the bottom of a well; they are not worthy of our note.

Take Japan, take any nation of the West; every nation is under the same heavens, illumined by the same Sun, enjoying the beauty of the same Moon, sharing the same ocean, breathing the same air, possessing the same human sentiments. Therefore, whatever we have in excess we should give to them, taking to us whatever they have in excess, teaching each other and learning together, never ashamed nor boastful, each fulfilling the needs of the other, mutually praying for the happiness of all. So, according to the reason of Heaven and the ways of man, a nation should hold mutual intercourse with all others, and when reason is against it, it should bow even before the black natives of Africa, and when reason is on its side, it should stand in defiance of the mighty warships of England and America, or when the honor of the country is at stake, every man in the whole nation should throw down his life to defend the glory of the country. Such should be the picture of a free and independent country.

But some people are like the Chinese, who thinks there is no nation in the world except his own, and whenever he meets some foreigners, he calls them barbarians as if they were beasts walking on four legs, despises and detests them, and simply endeavors to keep them out, never thinking of the real strength of his own country, with the result that he is subjected to humiliation by those "barbarians." All this indicates that he is ignorant of the proper limitations of a nation, exactly like a man who, not knowing the true meaning of freedom, falls into the evils of wayward-ness and licentiousness.

Since the return of the Imperial rule, Japan's system of govern-ment has come to be much changed. Externally she associates with the world under international law; internally she guides the people to an understanding of freedom and independence, permitting the plain people to take family names and to go on horseback, which one may consider the finest act of all times. One may say that the movement to make the four classes—samurai, farmer, artisan, and merchant—equal has here been placed on a firm footing.

Therefore, henceforth among the people of Japan there will be no such thing as the rank to which a man is born. Only by his ability and the position he holds will a man's rank be determined. For instance, it is proper to pay respect to a government official, but this is not the respect of the man himself. We should pay respect to the fact that he holds his position because of his ability and administers the precious laws for the benefit of the people. It is not the person that one is to respect; it is the law that one is to respect.

All people remember that during the Shōgun's regime the August Jar of Tea used to be carried along the Tōkaidō Highway. Not only the Jar of Tea but a hawk in the Shōgun's household was more precious than an ordinary man; when a horse of the Shōgun's household came by, all the travelers on the highway stood aside. Everything, even a piece of stone or tile, appeared awesome and precious when the words "belonging to the Shōgun" were attached to it. Though disliking it for many centuries, people had become used to it, and thus the ugly custom came to be. After all, this did not come from the dignity of the law, nor from the value of the things themselves; it was simply a cowardly device of the gov-ernment to show off its power and to restrict the freedom of the people. One may call it an empty pretense without substance.

Nowadays, as such miserable laws and customs are to be dis-continued throughout the country, people ought to set their hearts at ease, and if there should be the least complaint against the gov-ernment, they should never hold it against the officials in secret, but they should seek a proper channel to present the case and to argue about it quietly and without hesitation. If the case should be in accord with Heaven's reason and with humanity, one should fight for it even at the risk of one's own life. Such shall be the lot of a man who calls himself a citizen of a civilized nation.

As I have said before, an individual man and an individual nation are free and unrestricted according to Heaven-made law. And so, if this freedom of the nation is in jeopardy, one should not fear to stand against all the nations of the world; if one's individual freedom is in jeopardy, one should not stand in awe of even the government officials. Moreover, at the time when the equality of the four classes has been established, all men should feel secure in giving free rein to their activities as long as they follow the ways of Heaven. However, as every man has his position in society, he must have ability and virtue appropriate to his position. In order to give ability and virtue to oneself, one must learn the logic of things. In order to learn the logic of things, one must study his letters. This is the reason for the urgent need of learning.

As we look around today, the position of the three classes—farmer, artisan, and merchant—has advanced a hundred fold, and soon will be on a level with the samurai. Even now, the way has been opened for drawing talented men from among the three classes into government service. Therefore, all men must reflect upon themselves and realize that they now occupy a high position, and therefore must behave in a manner worthy of that position.

There is no one more pitiful and obnoxious than the ignorant and the illiterate. In the extreme of ignorance, they lose the sense of shame. When they grow poor and hungry because of their ignorance, they do not blame themselves, but they envy the rich, sometimes banding themselves to force a petition or even taking to armed rioting. Shall I call them shameless, or shall I call them lawless? They owe their security to the law of the nation and they carry on their household business under the law. They take advantage of it when they may. Yet, when their personal greed dictates, they break the law. Is this not an outrage on fair reason?

It sometimes happens that a well-established man with some means knows only how to accumulate money but is entirely ignorant in educating his children. Uneducated children will be foolish, which is not to be wondered at, and they will become lazy and licentious, finally squandering away like a wisp of smoke the for-

unknown factors. In computer programming terms, it boils down to expanding nested IF THEN ELSE clauses.

Suppose a vendor estimates originally that to code a processing logic, it takes, say, three logical questions. For example, suppose the case involves administering a health insurance program:

> Is the claimant an active employee?
>> If so, is the employee eligible to receive reimbursement?
>>> If so, has the employee's deductible been met?
>>>> If so, issue a check for the amount.

The vendor assumes such a set of questions will be adequate to process claims and estimates it will take about eight hours of computer programming time plus testing. The indentation is provided to show the nesting (a case within) effect.

In reality the situation turns out to be far more complex, and the work takes a lot longer.

What the system designer or programmer does not know are any additional test conditions he or she needs to include in the logic, say, regarding the beneficiary's claim date. If it is retroactive to the previous coverage, the coverage rule is different, and the payment calculation is different. That means the logic has to be modified and thoroughly checked for any other similar conditions. There was no way the programmer could have known about it because it was never documented clearly. Similar unforeseen and undocumented cases can pop up elsewhere.

Suppose such a discovery was made after the check was issued. Undoing an error like that is naturally very costly. It involves notifying those who received incorrect payments, reversing the database to the previous state, and catching up with the overall delays of the data processing that had to be halted to enable the correction.

Without thorough documentation, the vendor had no idea how complex the operation could get. The case faults those who were responsible for decision making for not assessing the extent of the knowledge transfer work, not properly auditing the quality of work, and proceeding without preventive or backup plans. Their cost-savings figures were now fictions.

This unknown and expanding logic is inherent in life. It is nearly impossible to document all cases so the knowledge can be transferred to someone else. Even when we have knowledge experts in the field, sometimes the experts themselves are caught off guard because it is nearly impossible to consider all the combinations of what-ifs. When contracts change, changes made are often great, and the impacting consequences cannot be assessed till later.

Thus we have (somewhat well-versed) experts and (relatively inexperienced) analysts in an environment that changes rapidly (especially in electronics) and drastically (like new contracts by different insurers), as the case in point. The resulting overrun in cost and time to modify the systems with appropriate increases in hardware power, training, and maintenance, to name a few, will be significant. This may well have been a case of "we did not know what we did not know."

In summary, as is known today, the outsourcing of activities that require expert know-how, as opposed to routine activities without such knowledge, needs careful review. Especially if the knowledge base is not well documented, that gap alone needs to be dealt with prior to outsourcing consideration. (In my personal experience, there was no dependable documentation because it was nearly impossible to spend money on the expensive resources needed to prepare it.) And the justification of outsourcing by cost alone is dangerous, especially if the cost is estimated on optimistic (or idealistic) assumptions. At the least, we need to have an alternative option so that we can avoid costly consequences. An impression is that outsourcing is often too hastily sought and justified mostly by cost savings in labor, which may in the end never be realized. Intangibles such as the quality of service and the loyalty to overall corporate mission are hard to handle, naturally, but the strength of the true goal attainment effort should blow away any short-term cost-reduction fads.

Appendix Four: We Could Use the Computer to Help Us Think Better

Here is a more enjoyable or new perspective on thinking.

If learning and thinking is tracing the old and exploring the new through trillions of links of words, then part of that activity, storing and retrieving, could be performed by the computer. Of course, in reality the computer needs instructions as to how to achieve that. My claim is that as long as it is possible to explain things in words, it is feasible to do so. Exactly what do I mean by that?

Well, the basic idea is not difficult to grasp.
Because we communicate in words, we can focus on them. The hard question is, how do we use them, in turn, for helping us think?

First, we number and identify each one, from number one to, say, two million, as they are listed in a dictionary, like *Webster's*.

Second, we organize the words by concept, much like the thesaurus, provided in groups of synonyms and antonyms.

We then start defining each word in terms of the conceptual organization, using the numbers we used in the dictionary. We can imagine a thesaurus defined in terms of those indices.

For example, let us consider the word *inverse*:
In the thesaurus, it appears under *contrariety* and *inversion*.
The definition of *inverse* in the dictionary is:
1. Opposite in order, nature or effect;
2. Being an inverse function

We can express these in terms of the indices and their links or "pointers."

Now, if we pose a question in definition (that is the "what" question), we can see that we are essentially looking for answers that can be represented in terms of links of words, or pointers consisting of defining indices.

If we pose a question in reason or logic (that is the "how" or "why" question), we can see that we are essentially looking for answers that can be represented in terms of links of words, or pointers consisting of reasoning indices.

So now we can surmise that these observations tie with the concept that learning is tracing of links and thinking is searching of links. In our jargon the links are the paths of those indices.

Such paths could be made efficient for tracing and searching with additional criteria, such as English grammar and our accumulated knowledge or experiences.

In learning the latter may be helpful; that is basically how we learn from infancy. But in thinking, we may be stifled by that. That is basically what we hear when new ideas and concepts are created. Regardless, the goal of the search will guide the search. It is important to select the right or highest goal.

If we imagine we are Gauss or Einstein, faced with a challenge to explain a certain phenomenon, we cannot match their ability to search for paths, for such reasons as the enormity of selections for paths and lack of basic information or knowledge. But if we had that capacity to store and recall them via the computer, would we not be able to keep pace with how the geniuses think? Wouldn't we be able to inspire and imagine far and deep to see beautiful patterns of prime numbers or reach an outlandish perspective?

We may not know the answer quickly, but today we can be sure that it is plausible. At least the mathematics of the idea seem feasible. We already have tools such as tags and the universal record locators (URLs) that we use in HTML on the web or the Internet. And our five-step approach can facilitate these efforts well in that we continuously endeavor to build character and intelligence.

Hopefully someday we will be able to test these ideas.

Appendix Five: Useful Troubleshooting Tips

If the fun in learning and thinking is gone, here is a troubleshooting kit or a "cheat sheet" to regain the footage for getting back on the right track.

First as a reminder, the Five Steps of Learning How to Think are:

1. **Observe** details, as in "**What** on earth do I have here?" Let neurons carry the messages freely.
2. **Ask** simple and brief questions to force easy answers. Start firing up neurons to get a hold of easy paths.
3. **Confirm** goals and purposes, as in, "**Why** on earth do I want this?" Identify the furthest targets as the final destinations of the paths.
4. **Discover** reasons and criteria for paths, as in "**How** on earth can I get there?" Be creative in selecting specific paths.
5. **Review** your performance for growth, as in, "**I want to keep learning**!" Remember the search history, and learn from it to enhance the quality of your character.

Generally, to achieve the steps, I go through the following diagnostic checklist:
- Is my overall health OK to take on the challenge?
- Do I know how to do it, how to think, or how to proceed?
- Am I sure about my goal being the "highest" I can aim for?
- Are my questions simple and direct toward my goal?
- Am I enjoying my effort?

As it is very common to find it hard to do any of these and stay on the right track, I have provided the following set of troubleshooting tips as a helpful guide. The list is meant to serve as a self-diagnosis tool. When I am lost, more often than not I find it useful and do emerge from the maze rather victoriously. By victorious I mean I not only succeed in fixing the trouble but also often find other how-to approaches that are much more fun than the original approach!

Tips for Troubleshooting General "Lack of Fun"

Step	Area	Common Symptoms	Sample Rescue Actions for Learning or Thinking	Neural Network Aspect
Preliminary Preparation Step	**Health:** physical, mental	Not enjoying it	Pause; reassess the approach	Reboot
		Feel tired, sleepy	Pause; decide on rest or discipline	Reinitialize
	Environment: mentor, ambience	It's noisy	Use logical chain to shut out; reroute energy to main task	Tune up
		Not up to it	Review goals and purpose	
		Stressed out	Clear one at a time, perform exercise, listen to music, reset expectation	
		Not confident	Recall confidence, positivity, optimism	
		It's too complicated	Clear the impression, perception	
		Not willing, predisposed or biased	Be humble. Listen to others	
		Headache	Stop, decide to rest or abort, be honest, acknowledge, laugh	
		Angry, short, impatient, or upset	Pause, acknowledge each path link, refocus on the task	
		Don't like the mentor	Review goals, purpose and approach, check attitude	

Step	Area	Common Symptoms	Sample Rescue Actions for Learning or Thinking	Neural Network Aspect
	Observe	It's blurry It's too complicated It's too hard	* Break down into small pieces * Elucidate * Check to see if I am missing anything * Compare * Be more attentive * Undo predispositions * Listen to others	Fire up neurons and neurotransmitters Turn on receptors
Execution Step	**Ask**	Don't know where or how to start Don't know what to ask	* Get curious * Ask simple, short 5W1H questions * Challenge statements * Refute beliefs * Start with new assumptions * Break convention * Force Q&A * Paraphrase * Listen to what others are saying	Begin search for paths Chain small paths
	Confirm	Not sure why I need to learn or think	* Review purpose * Rekindle motivation * Reaffirm goals * Check the ethics * Set goals high * Pay closer attention to my diction, elucidation, and other details * Ensure questions and goal compatible * Is this what I truly want? * Honor own decisions	Check paths to the destinations Use the integrity criteria

Strategy Step			
Discover	Don't know how to go about Feel I am done	* Discard what was learned * Prove * Ask why (strategic), how (logistic), what (tactical) * Ask what-ifs * Check for any other cases * Turn each stone * It does not "have to" be * Check if it is working for me * Recall ethics and standards * Listen to what others are saying * Imagine * Be creative * Go up on the elevator for a high-level view * My aim or goal needs review	Extend and explore Trace the process paths
Review	**Feel I am not growing** **Little hunger for learning** **Having no fun**	Identify knowledge improvement Review results Recall lessons learned Identify character improvement Pay closer attention to my diction, elucidation, and other details Check consistency Evaluate own performance Make sure whether I really want to improve or not Be honest	Assess the health of the infrastructure Feed vitality to grow and evolve Check for enthusiasm and pleasure

Index

tunes inherited from their ancestors. To rule such foolish men, reason will not do; the only way will be to keep them in order by the show of force. A proverb of the West says, "Over foolish people, there is a harsh government." It is not that the government is harsh of itself; it is the foolish people who bring harshness upon themselves. If the government over foolish people is harsh, reason requires that the government over wise people should be good. Therefore, in our country, too, we have this kind of government because there is this kind of people.

Should our people ever sink into deeper ignorance and illiteracy, the government will become even severer than today. Should people turn their minds to learning, acquire an understanding of logic, and advance toward civilization, the government will move toward freedom and leniency. The severity or leniency of the government are natural consequences of the worth or unworthiness of the people themselves. Who in the world would prefer harsh rule to good rule? Who would not pray for strength and fortune for his own country? Who would welcome humiliation from foreigners? These are human sentiments common to all.

In this age, for those who have the mind to serve their country, there are no problems urgent enough to worry the mind and torture the body. The important thing for everyone for the present is that he should regulate his conduct according to humanity, and apply himself earnestly to learning in order to absorb a wide knowledge and to develop abilities worthy of his position. This will make it easy for the government to rule and pleasant for the people to accept its rule, every man finding his place and all playing a part in preserving the peace of the nation. This should be the only aim. The encouragement of learning that I advocate, too, takes this for its aim.

Appendix Three: Complexity of Knowledge Transfer for Outsourcing

This Appendix might be hard to comprehend if the reader is not familiar with the type of thinking in computer programming. Computer programming is based on rules and instructions that the programmer is attempting to lay out or code in the computer programming language. That means the rules need to be understood clearly by the programmer. In most cases that is possible. On other occasions it is not possible because the situation is not definable due to lack of precedence or knowledge. It is simply those cases of "not known or experienced yet." If the programmer attempts to go ahead and code a set of instructions in such a case, the program will probably crash as it is not instructed to handle it. The danger is that businesses often do not have time to investigate these unknowns thoroughly and risk taking the path toward failure. Better learning and thinking here warn us that we need to set expectations appropriately and be prepared to face unexpected unknowns.

In the effort to transfer "knowledge" or a set of instructions for what to do in different situations to an outsourcer or an organization outside of the corporation under consideration, the complexity can be underestimated. The underestimation can then become a cause for delay of implementation of the transfer effort. The contents here could appear to be technical, but the essence is that basically the logic involved should not contain any hidden information or surprises. Otherwise it will take a lot longer to explain the logic.

Delays of projects have been treated previously in an elegant book by Frederick P. Brooks. [60] We will focus here specifically on the

---

60 Frederick P. Brooks, Jr., *The Mythical Man-Month* (Reading, PA: Addison-Wesley, 1982).

Bibliography

Abreu, Anthony. *"How Did Eratosthenes Measure the Circumference of the Earth?"*. July 3, 2012. http://todaslascosasdeanthony. com/2012/07/03/eratosthenes-earth-circumference/ (accessed January 23, 2014).

Alfred, Randy. *Wired, "June 19, 240 B.C.: The Earth Is Round, and It's This Big".* www.wired.com, Retrieved 2013-06-22 (accessed June 19, 2008).

andrewacton100. *"Bo Diddley," YouTube video.* www.youtube.com/ watch?v=zpvkq9n5604 (accessed March 17, 2012).

Bard, Arthur S. Bard and Mitchell G. *The Complete Idiot's Guide to Understanding the Brain.* Alpha Books, 2002.

Bartlett, John. *Familiar Quotations.* Little, Brown & Company, 1968.

Barzun, Jacques. *Begin Here.* University of Chicago Press, 1992.

—. *From Dawn to Decadence.* Harper Perennial, 2000.

—. *Simple and Direct.* Harper Perennial, 2001.

Bell, E. T. *Men of Mathematics.* Simon and Schuster, 1965.

BrainyQuotes, BookRags Media Network. *BrainyQuotes, s.v. "Buddha".* www.brainyquote.com/quotes/authors/b/buddha.html (accessed October 4, 2011).

Clark, Jim. *Chemguide.* November 2012. www.chemguide.co.uk/basicorg/conventions/names.html (accessed January 23, 2014).

Committee, Physical Science Study. *Physics.* Heath and Company, 1960.

David Rubel, ed. *The Bedside Baccalaureate* . Agincourt Press Book, 2008.

Descartes, Rene. *Discourse on Method.* The Liberal Arts Press, Inc., 1976.

Frankl, Viktor E. *Man's Search for Meaning.* Touchstone Books, 1984.

Frederick C. Mish, Editor in Chief. *Webster's Ninth New Collegiate Dictionary.* Merriam-Webster Inc., 1983.

Fukuzawa, Yukichi. *The Autobiography of Yukichi Fukuzawa.* Columbia University Press, 1968.

Gallo, Isaac Moreno. "Roman Surveying, Nov. 3–6, 2004, translated by Brian R. Bishop." http://www.trainanvs.net/pdfs/surveying.pdf (accessed March 30, 2010).

Gleason, H. A. *An Introduction to Descriptive Linguistics.* Holt, Rinehart and Winston, 1961.

Isaacson, Walter. *Einstein: His Life and Universe.* Simon and Schuster., 2007.

Journal, The Wall Street. "Deming's Demons, Workplace in Managing Change Section." (The Wall Street Journal) 1990.

Kaizuka Shigeki, Iwatomo Fujino, Shinobu Ono, Ed.,. *Kadokawa Kanwa Chujiten.* Kadokawa Publishing Company, 1963.

Lowe, Janet. *Bill Gates Speaks.* John Wiley and Sons, Inc., 1998.

Ogata, Mitsuo. *Engineers' Manual of Probability and Statistical Methods.* Cummins Engine Company, 1975.

Palmateer, Jake. *Daily Star.* January 22, 2008. www.thedailystar.com/local/local_story_023040035 (accessed October 17, 2013).

Pauk, Walter. *How to Study in College, Fifth Edition.* Houghton Mifflin Company, 1993.

Perrin, Noel. *Giving Up the Gun: Japan's Reversion to the Sword, 1543–1879* . David R. Godine, Publisher, Inc., 1979.

Plauger, Brian W. Kernighan and P. J. *The Elements of Programming Style.* McMillan, 1998.

an ordinary carriage. He joined the first Japanese mission to Europe in 1862, visiting the capitals of all the countries with which Japan had concluded treaties in 1858. The mission's hosts always took pains to show them the most impressive examples of western civilization that their countries could muster, and Fukuzawa, an indefatigable note-taker, lost no opportunity of learning and marking all he could.

He returned to Japan to find that assassins were abroad ready to strike down foreigners or any Japanese suspected of pro-foreign leanings. For many years Fukuzawa did not dare to go out at night. Instead he stayed at home, taught in his school, and started to write the books which were soon to make him famous.

The most celebrated of these was *Seiyō Jijō* (Things Western), which in 1866 sold no less than 250,000 copies, an unprecedented number for those days. Its immense success was due to the fact that it gave the Japanese public exactly the information about the West that it needed. A few intrepid spirits might have studied works on western chemistry, medicine, or gunnery, but hardly anyone had any conception of how the people in the West lived their everyday lives, what they wore and ate, and how they were governed. *Seiyō Jijō* described western hospitals, schools and newspapers, museums, the taxation system, and other ordinary social institutions. It gave the Japanese public for the first time a picture of what the western countries were like to live in.

Its success was so great that soon all books about the West came to be called *Fukuzawa-bon*. But even then its author could not believe that the knowledge it imparted would ever prove of lasting value and importance. "I had

his fellows to expend such selfless energy on the study of Dutch science? It was not the hope of fame or gain. No one at that time saw in them the future leaders of the new Japan, the pioneers of the intellectual and political movement which was to result in the momentous changes of the Meiji period. Rather they appeared to the rest of their countrymen as weird and disagreeable eccentrics, given to disgusting practices which put them on a par with the outcast *eta*. Their only incentive at that time, Fukuzawa tells us, was the pleasure of acquiring rare and difficult knowledge. Knowledge desirable not because it was likely to prove useful, but simply because it was difficult. It was as though they were swallowing a nasty medicine, not because it was likely to do them any good, but simply because they were the only people brave enough to swallow it.

Several more years were to elapse, indeed, before Fukuzawa in any way began to realize the potential importance of the studies he had undertaken. They were years, however, full of adventure and momentous events. He was summoned to Edo by the clan authorities to start a school for the study of Dutch. He visited the foreign trading community in Yokohama, to make the disheartening discovery that no one there spoke Dutch or understood anything he said. Nothing daunted, he made up his mind at once to set about the even more formidable task of learning English. He joined the first Japanese mission to America in 1860, sailing through atrocious weather to San Francisco. There, he tells us, he was bored by explanations of the process of galvanizing and the use of the vacuum in sugar refining, which he had understood perfectly for years, but utterly puzzled by such things as

Reed Smith, William Paxton and Basil G. Meserve. *Learning to Write.* Heath and Company , 1963.

Regis, Ed. "The Forgotten Code Cracker." (Scientific American, Inc.) 2007.

Remington, Carolyn Lyon. *Vibrant Silence.* The Lawyers Co-operative Publishing Company, 1965.

Reynolds, Garr. *Presentation Zen.* New Riders, 2008.

Sacks, Oliver. *Musicophilia.* Alfred A. Knopf, 2007.

Smith, Arthur Rockwell. *The Game of Go.* Charles E. Tuttle Company, 1908.

Timothy Ferris, Ed. *The World Treasury of Physics, Astronomy and Mathematics.* Little Brown and Company, 1991.

Twain, Mark. *Innocents Abroad.* 1869.

Wang, An. *Lessons, an autobiography.* New York: Addison-Wesley Publishing Company, Inc., 1986.

White, W. Strunk and E. B. *The Elements of Style.* McMillan, 1979.

Wikipedia. *Wikipedia, "Coriolis Effect".* http://en.wikipedia.org/wiki/Coriolis_effect (accessed January 6, 2014).

—. *Wikipedia, s.v. "A. Rodin,".* en.wikipedia.org/wiki/Auguste_Rodin (accessed December 27, 2013).

—. *Wikipedia, s.v. "Eratosthenes".* en.wikipedia.org/wiki/Eratosthenes (accessed December 23, 2013).

—. *Wikipedia, s.v. "Romaji".* en.wikipedia.org/wiki/Romaji (accessed January 5, 2014).

The test and the use of a human being's education is that he finds plea-sure in the exercise of his mind.

—Jacques Barzun, *Begin Here: The Forgotten Conditions of Teaching and Learning*